HANDING BACK
CONTROL

A Journey Toward Freedom

RUTH EMBERY

Handing Back Control: A journey toward freedom

Copyright © 2015 Ruth Embery

Second Edition © 2022

All rights reserved. No part of this publication may be reproduced, stored in, or introduced into a retrieval system, or transmittted, in any form, or by any means (electronic, mechanical, photocopying, recording or otherwise) without the prior written permission of the publisher. Thank you for respecting the hard work of this author.

Published by: Voice in the Dark Publishing, Melbourne, Australia

ISBN: 978-0-6453488-2-8 (Print)

ISBN: 978-0-6453488-3-5 (Electronic)

Unless otherwise noted, all Scripture quotations are taken from THE HOLY BIBLE, NEW INTERNATIONAL VERSION® NIV®
Copyright © 1973, 1978, 1984 by International Bible Society®
Used by permission. All rights reserved worldwide.
Scripture quotations marked AMP are taken from the Amplified® Bible, Copyright © 1954, 1958, 1962, 1964, 1965, 1987 by The Lockman Foundation
Used by permission. (www.Lockman.org)
Cover photo steering wheel: © Dyudin Stanislav/Shutterstock.com
Cover design: © Ruth Embery

Dedication

This book is dedicated to every *control freak* out there, particularly those who are not yet aware of it. May you find the freedom and abundance that comes with letting go.

"I came that they may have and enjoy life, and have it in abundance (to the full, till it overflows)."

(John 10:10, AMP)

"Whoever wants to save his life will lose it, but whoever loses his life for me will find it."

(Matt 16:25)

— *Jesus*

Contents

Acknowledgements	i
Preface	iii
Introduction	vii
Handing Back Control of What I Have	1
Handing Back Control of Others	17
Handing Back Control of My Future	31
Handing Back Control of God	49
Handing Back Control of the World	65
Handing Back Control of Offence	74
Handing Back Control of Structure	79
Handing Back Control of My Reputation	89
Life Restored	98
Conclusion	107
Postscript	109
About the Author	113
Also by Ruth Embery	114
About Voice in the Dark Publishing	115

Acknowledgements

I would like to thank the many friends who have encouraged me to write over the years, particularly those who seeded the thought that I could write a book. Of course, the major contributor in the department of encouragement has been my cherished husband, Martin, whose almost blasé confidence in my ability and what I have to say has often been all that has kept me at it. I would further like to acknowledge his help and patience with the endless iterations of the cover design. Thanks also to my helpful friends, David Gallus and Helen Damster for donating their time and abilities to proof read and edit. It almost goes without saying that I also give thanks to God, without whom I would have no story to write. To Him be the glory.

It has been a long time coming, but here it is.

Preface
"He's not a tame lion"[1]

I stood at the top of the hill, hoping desperately that this was the last one. Several arguments were running around in my head. I was sorely tempted to give up. I was tired and aching all over. The fear that I am getting old and past it flashed through my mind. Not that I am a quitter, but I am heading for middle age now... No! It is simply the lack of exercise over the last couple of months that had reduced my fitness to about its lowest ever. I contemplated the hill again. It was a long way to the bottom.

One voice started telling me that I would probably fall over at the point where there was a bit of a hillock. Either that or where the trail started to turn. Maybe even both. Another voice told me "So what? You can get back up again." But I was sincerely starting to doubt the truth of that. A louder voice yelled back "Don't be so negative! If you think about falling over, of course you will. Self-fulfilling prophecy. Decide you won't fall over, be confident."

My husband, Martin, and I were having one of our rare weekends when our blended parental responsibilities were at their other parents' homes and we were free to have some us time. It was the first weekend of the ski season (actually, of a couple of ski seasons) where there was enough snow to ski and we were free! We had

---

[1] Extract from *The Lion, The Witch And The Wardrobe* by CS Lewis © copyright CS Lewis Pty Ltd 1950.

bought ourselves cross country skis a couple of years back, but the snow season had been so abysmal the last year we really hadn't got out and used them much. It seemed a God-given opportunity, one of those times where I felt that God had unaccountably and wonderfully blessed us. The snow report said "Excellent for XC skiing on groomed trails". The weather was beautiful, with clear blue skies and no wind. There are really no better conditions for a day out in the Australian bush skiing. However, at this point I was beginning to wonder whether God had blessed me, or whether He was actually having a great laugh at my expense.

As I continued to study the features of the hill, taking off my skis and walking it was starting to look good. But then it would take so much longer than skiing it, even if I did fall over. And I would probably only fall over once. Martin had skied ahead. I had told him to. He was full of supportive comments and instructions, but I was past it. I think he had realised it was time to leave me to my inefficient and pain inducing self. In fact, he was probably starting to get concerned at this point and wondering if he needed to come to rescue me. It was time to make a decision and move. I would do it. I was getting better and if I could just maintain my snowplough, I would be fine. Time to stop thinking and get on with it. All the instructions went through my mind as a checklist as I perched at the edge of the slope. Bend your knees, keep your back straight, weight over your heels. I used my stocks to push myself forward.

The first stretch, I managed to keep my speed in check and my body under control. I tried to focus on just a little way ahead, occasionally glancing further along to be prepared for what was to come. I was doing ok. I was ok. Just as I began to relax, there were some bumps on the trail. I tensed and started to stress. My hips locked agonisingly and I had to shift position. And it was all downhill from there! My speed increased to out of control; I started to lose my balance. Out of nowhere, my arms and stocks began to flail wildly as I madly tried to make my body obey. Needless to say, I found myself, once more, face first in the snow, legs at unusual angles, although nothing damaged except my pride. I lay there for a while, wondering why it was so easy to lie in the snow, but so hard to want to get up again and hoping no one would come down behind me. Whether they were equally out of control and I would have to desperately try to get out of the way, or whether they were of that variety of people who look at you with pity as they glide by with confidence and ease, I was not in the mood.

I did eventually make it back to the car park without having to remove my skis. As much as I was struggling, I love cross-country skiing and will go back for more. I just wish that I could make my body do what it needs to, because that would mean that I would ski so much better and come home in far better shape.

Reflecting on the information I have gleaned (though not mastered) about cross-country skiing, I see my experience as a life illustration. It shows me how holding on to control too tightly causes me pain and grief. Learning to let go of my fear, and trying to do things differently, even when they feel all wrong is just as relevant for my life as my skiing.

Living in Western society, my observation is that we hold a belief that we should be able to do whatever we want to do if we just focus on it and try hard enough. From soap operas, to lifestyle programs, magazines and movies, a variety of media bombards us with stories about people who have beaten the odds and succeeded to achieve something they wanted to. There seems to be a component of our society, and even within some of the church, that sees life being all about self-actualisation – the idea that we each have potential; that life is about finding what our potential is in our particular set of abilities and maximising it. On the surface, this may seem very positive, but I suggest that it can hold us back because it can keep us focussed on ourselves and our own abilities alone.

As a Christian I have been increasingly aware of some of the issues involved with this way of thinking. I have come to a place where I realise that self-fulfilling is not always as fulfilling as we think and that our journey of life in faith is far more satisfactory as increasingly *less of me, more of Jesus*. Although this idea used to fill me with fear of loss, I am seeing that it is not as unbearable as I once thought. I am not missing out on half of life. I am not losing myself in a negative sense, and it is certainly never boring or prohibitive. Letting go of the belief that I can control the outcomes of my life is not as scary as I once thought. Actually, it is quite the opposite, and the freedom I have gained, I would never exchange for anything the world can offer. This is my story of that journey so far.

Introduction

Few people I know would admit to being control freaks. Equally as few of us enjoy feeling like our lives are out of control. However, there will be times in most lives where circumstances will occur that leave us feeling exactly that: out of control. If 2020 and 2021 have shown us anything, it is exactly how little influence we really have over our lives. How we deal with situations we have no control over depends on our wiring as well as our beliefs about the world, ourselves and God.

One of my favourite pictures from the Bible comes from Ezekiel 47, where Ezekiel finds himself led by a man along and through a river that brings life wherever it goes, even into the Dead Sea. Reading about Ezekiel travelling through water that is at first ankle deep, then knee deep, waist deep and finally to water that is so deep you would need to swim, that no one could cross, creates an image that resonates profoundly with me. I see this river reflecting life in God. We can go in ankle deep, and get some blessing and enjoyment. We can even go knee deep, where the impact is a little more noticeable. At waist deep, the effects are starting to get significant. However, if we really want to feel the full force of life in God, we need to jump into the deep and allow His current to take us where it will, at the pace it will, even to flood over our heads and overwhelm us. The parallel with baptism and dying to self is quite clear, but far from throwing us in the deep end, God always holds His hand out with an invitation to let go and experience an ever increasing measure of His abundance.

Even though I really love the idea of jumping into the deep with God, there are plenty of times where I get a little scared of where it might take me, get a little afraid that I am crazy and have lost the plot, or even fear of the consequences of where it might lead me. I may lose everything I value. This is not how an educated, intelligent, rational person should behave, and so I return back to where it feels safer. I like to think that I am ready to make the leap, and maybe, step by step I am getting deeper in my relationship with God; maybe there will come a time when I will be so busy focusing on God that I won't notice how deep the water is anymore.

My experience with God, so far, has taught me that He is reliable, and whether we see the floods as life giving or destroying, I do believe He is faithful to carry us through. Though this story is not prescriptive, or instructional, my hope and prayer is that it will encourage you that God is faithful, trustworthy and true to His promises and that when He promises to give us abundant life, He does just that. We simply have to decide what we are prepared to let go of in order to take hold of His life. Like a drowning person, we have to decide whether it is worth the risk of letting go of the piece of flotsam that is barely holding our weight in order to grab on to something that sometimes feels a little phantom; something that we only seem to get little glimpses of in a rough and stormy sea. We must decide, at some point, whether we are done with battling on in our own strength, or we are ready to trust Jesus at His word.

The topics I have covered here are those that stand out for me. Yours might be different. Your experience of God's grace in these areas will surely be different. I have started with finances and possessions because this is an area that impacts every person on the planet. Unless we rely on the goodness of a large number of other people, it is very difficult to operate in this world without some form of working for reward, whether that is through cash or goods and services. The way we manage this aspect will very much determine the direction of our lives. Jesus addressed this issue directly when He said that we cannot serve God and mammon (which translates as riches or wealth). Deciding which of these is more important to us will unequivocally determine the life path we take.

I hope you enjoy journeying with me, and pray that God's Holy Spirit will open His truths to you ever deeper, both as you continue to read and throughout your life. For those who would like to dive in deeper for yourselves, there are a few questions at the end of each chapter.

Handing Back Control of What I Have

"The Lord is my Shepherd, I shall not be in want" Ps 23:1
"And my God shall supply all your needs according to His great riches in Christ Jesus." Phil 4:19

I grew up in a large family living on the single income of a teacher. While we were never massively well off, I don't think we felt excessively poor, either, even though there were times we didn't feel we had a great deal compared to some of our friends. There were plenty of instances where we made do with what we had, and much of what we had was hand-me-downs, goods that others no longer needed, we bought second hand or were simply homemade. However, an aspect cocooned within my upbringing that I am quite sure I don't fully appreciate, is the gift my parents gave me as they instilled certain assumptions about giving into their kids.

My parents modelled giving through the way they lived. We saw them give at church each week. They not only gave money but also their time and abilities. There was no fuss or ceremony about this; it was just what you did. They also gave of their time both inside and outside church. I remember occasions of walking the streets with my mother as she door-knocked for such groups as "Freedom from Hunger". They often reminded us of our wealth compared to many other people around the world. My parents also tried to make this very practical. One Christmas we had a Vietnamese refugee family come and share the day with us, which was very confronting! Among other things, my mother also spent some time helping a single mother who had no car, taking her shopping and trying to help her to budget and my father did some work as a parole officer, helping young men re-enter the community.

The modelling and instruction in these types of actions and attitudes through normal life, helped me to find giving relatively easy. I have never questioned doing it and cannot imagine not giving. Along the way, I will admit that I picked up some unintentional negative messages where I have felt I didn't deserve much. There were also times of rebellion against my parents, particularly with the incentive to eat food I was not particularly fond of: "Be grateful! People in such and such a country would be happy to get anything"! I vividly remember my very defiant response at one point: "Well, get an envelope and we'll send it to them!" However, within all this mix, there has never been a question in my mind about whether to give. It is a given!

Somewhere along the way, however, my attitude to giving had a subtle but significant shift. Two things stand out in my memory.

The first was an introduction to the concept of tithing (giving ten percent of my income to God's work here on earth). We did not go to a church denomination where tithing was taught and it was not a principle I was aware my parents engaged with. At a Bible study group I attended in my teens, though, I was taught this as a Biblical principle. The message was probably not as legalistic as it might have sounded, but the impression was that this is what God expects of us, this is how we showed our gratitude to God for what He has already given us.

Around this time, I was at a conference with a further message was on giving. This really cemented an attitude or belief in my heart that has become so real that I cannot imagine seeing the concept any other way. The point the speaker made that has stuck with me was a deeper way of seeing tithing. He reminded us that everything we have is from God and by His grace, not because we have done anything to deserve it. As the Creator, He is the Source of all, from the physical world, to our abilities to work and create, to our emotional wellbeing. We cannot claim *anything* we have as our own. The speaker suggested that the way God saw things was that He only asked us to give Him a small portion of all He had given us for His work and the rest we were to spend on celebrating the life He had given us. Now, how I interpret that and what I might do with that remaining figure is in a continual state of flux, but somewhere around this time, I came to a place where I knew, without a doubt, that I was actually accountable to God for the way I spend every cent that comes my way.

Over the years I have had times where I have struggled to accept that He is pleased for me to spend money on really celebrating life, whether that be good food, clothes that celebrate my femininity or simply enjoying life. It is an area in which I have grown in understanding and yet one where I think everyone will have a different experience dependent on their unique journey.

More recently I have also come to see that our giving is a way to show our trust in God that He will continue to provide for us. Our attitudes and actions in giving keep us in a place where we can make thoughtful decisions about what we do with our money, rather than allowing money to control our lives. I believe the principle of tithing helps us to prevent money ruling our lives and reminds us that God is our Provider.

My understanding about financial giving has continued to grow. A further idea I heard was to see a tithe as the starting point. For someone on a low income, that may be all they can do. However, the suggestion was that as our income increases, our expenses do not necessarily grow at the same rate. If I am a single professional, my living expenses may not be much different to a single person working in a low wage position or to a student. In that position, I can give a great deal more. The most important part of this principle, though, was about my relationship with God. If my giving, at any point, is about getting in the *good books* with God, rather than coming from my gratitude to Him and wanting to partner with Him in what He is doing in the world, then I need to re-examine my motives.

Giving can be difficult. On a low or even non-existent income, it can be really hard to give out of what you don't have. There have been occasions in my life where not giving might have made some sense. However, I have found these have been opportunities where God has proven Himself faithful and I have got to know more of Him. My faith has grown through the tough times.

In my early twenties, I moved out of home. I was tired of travelling an hour and a half each way to university and besides, I felt ready to go it alone. I moved into a house with four other Christians and we had a great time. As I was still studying, however, it was a test of my financial resources. My parents didn't have the income to support me out of home, but I had worked full time for about four months over summer and saved hard. This gave me some capital to live off, with the view to getting a part time job down the track if I needed to.

Moving out of home, I had let church attendance lapse. This was not because my faith had changed, but largely due to my struggle between what I thought the Church *should* look like and the reality and disappointment with what I had experienced. I was still involved with Christian activities, though, and about half way through the year was at a Youth For Christ rally. They were looking for people to commit to just $10 a month to help support their ministry. At that time, my finances were diminishing rapidly and I was looking for work. However, I felt God nudge me. As I wasn't attending a church anywhere regularly I hadn't been giving, so I decided that this would be my place to give. I felt that God was saying *"Put me to the test. You honour me with your giving and I will supply your needs."* I made the commitment. Within days I was offered a fantastic part time job around the corner from university, a couple of hours each day, which they were happy for me to fit in with my schedule.

Shortly after this, another incident reinforced the message. Although the part time job was keeping my head above water, it was only just. I knew I had a cheque due from the taxation department as I had paid more tax than I needed when I was working fulltime over summer, but I was not sure when it would arrive. Sharing this with my mother as I spent some time at home during semester break, she offered me some money to tide me over. I could repay her as soon as my cheque came. I reluctantly accepted. It was with great joy that I arrived back at my abode to find the cheque from the taxation department awaiting me!

I would also like to highlight here, though, that by no means was I *just scraping by* financially. As much as I believe that God's blessings are not simply material blessings, I do believe that He likes to give us good things, which may be different according to our level of maturity or our need at the time. He is generous and abundant in His giving, and I don't think He wants His children to live in a stingy way. He gives to us in abundance to teach us to also give in abundance. For me, at this time, it meant that I not only had money to do the things I needed to do, but also to do things for pleasure, which included things like a new dress for my graduation ball.

Years later, after living this principle of giving since my teens, the lessons about my finances went to a new level. Although I felt like I was better off than many I knew in similar circumstances, as a single parent on the government pension, cash flow was often tight. I came to a point in time where I found myself stressed about how I would juggle the bills quite regularly. I also became aware that I was taking my stress out on my daughter, getting snappy with her interruptions as I was performing mental gymnastics with my finances.

As I stepped back, apologising to her and explaining why I was so frazzled, I had a memory from my childhood. It was a time where my parents were also struggling to pay the bills. I remembered the fear and anxiety that stuck with me for many years afterward and this hit me hard. It was not that my parents talked about their financial problems with us, I think I simply overheard them talking. When I had talked to my mother about this memory years later, she said that it had only been a very short period of time and had not been that much of an issue. However, as a young child, I had taken it on board and had great concern over this. I didn't want my daughter to feel like that. What could I do to ensure we weren't in that position?

At the same time, a verse of Scripture had been ringing in my ears for some time: *"You do not have because you do not ask"* (James 4:2).

Although others have challenged me that this verse can be interpreted in a distorted fashion to mean that we can get anything we want by simply asking God, I have also learnt that God will use whatever He needs to get our attention and to remind us of His promises to us. God does promise to meet our needs (for example, Matt 6:25-34) and I believe that He wants us to be dependent on Him. Jesus says that unless we become like little children we will never enter the Kingdom of Heaven (Mat 18:3). Little children are very dependent on their parents for everything. They trust implicitly and expect great things. We are to be like this with God. He wants us to seek Him for the answers to every area of our lives.

When I finally realised that God was trying to get my attention with this verse, that it was a message from my loving Heavenly Father, I made the rather obvious step forward and actually prayed about my finances, asking God to provide that which I needed. Some may wonder why I didn't pray about this earlier. I think this reflects the belief I had that because my needs were not as great as others', it felt like a selfish prayer.

A few days later, I had a phone call from my daughter's Godparents, who were living in Edinburgh, Scotland at the time. They had been praying about how they could help me, feeling distant and remote from my struggles after my marriage breakdown, but wanting to do something. They rang to find out my bank account number, because, after praying, they had decided that they would like to help me financially, by paying for my daughter's kindergarten fees. They were not aware at that time that my struggles were also financial. Of course, after my prayers, I could do nothing but accept! Furthermore, while I thought that they would make four payments, term by term, it was a great surprise to find they had put the whole amount into my account straight away. The benefit of this was that it got me over that hurdle of not quite having enough in the months where there were more bills.

I learnt my lesson well, this time! From then on, rather than trying to sort things out in my own strength, I realised that it was okay to ask for God's help and that He would actually help me. I ended up getting casual administration work with a company and it was extraordinary the number of times that I would get a phone call from them out of the blue, asking me to work, just when I needed it. At first it was often within a day of me praying, but later it got to the point where I hardly had to think about it and I'd get a call to work. I would like to stress here, though, that I don't believe that I should simply keep spending and expect God to pick up the tab. I need to be a good steward of what He provides for me. Having a budget can help, although being too rigid and stressed about exactly meeting it can be just as defeating – I can rely too much on my ability to meet my budget, and stop relying on God to meet my needs. I think that, like most things in life, there needs to be a balance.

I have not come to the end of my lessons about God's supply for my finances, though. Sometimes I struggle (and this has been a struggle all my adulthood), with the fact that, as an Australian, I am incredibly wealthy. We live in a country that has so much. Because of this, asking God for material needs continues to challenge me at times.

Over the past few years, my understanding and views about this have expanded and deepened, most particularly around the idea of God's reasons to bless us. Malachi 3:10 says, *"'Bring the whole tithe into the storehouse that there may be food in my house. Test Me in this,' says the Lord Almighty, 'and see if I will not throw open the floodgates of heaven and pour out so much blessing that you will not have room enough for it.'"* I have heard this passage used many times to encourage people to give.

While I would agree wholeheartedly with the belief or understanding of who God is for us, a God of abundance and generosity, it bothers me that an underlying message here may be that we can manipulate God. If I give, He will give even more back. Our giving needs to demonstrate our heart: our gratitude to God for *all* He has *already* supplied; a demonstration of our trust in His goodness towards us and His ability to provide all our needs (and more!); and a heart of kindness, mercy and love towards others in their need.

Someone once told me she had a problem with giving because she often gave more than she could afford and then couldn't pay her bills. I have thought about that often, having had the privilege of travelling and sharing with Christians in countries where they have far less than us. Rather, it has led me to wonder how much I can afford *not* to give. I have come to a position, though, where I realise that God places genuine needs before me and my willingness to respond is quite a good measure of the state of my heart. Learning to discern what is genuine and what is my responsibility is the tough part!

Another aspect of giving came from a greater understanding of promises in the Bible. In particular, the promise from God to Abram in Genesis 12:2-3 contains two parts. The first was that God would bless him and the second part was that all nations would be blessed through him. The idea here is that God doesn't bless us just to make us feel and look good. He doesn't bless us so we can have a cushy life. His blessings that He loves to pour down on us can also be a test. Will we simply keep them to ourselves and get *fat*, or do we use them to bless others, to be the answer to their prayers? This marries in with my increasing understanding, and sometimes frustration, about what it means to be part of the Body of Christ. Our role is to be Jesus to every person who comes across our path. We are to use all the blessings (our finances, material goods, time, energy, spiritual gifts, experiences in life) God has given us to pass something on to others in need.

In my journey, however, time passed, and I was challenged at a deeper level again about God's promise to meet my financial needs.

A couple of years after I remarried, we came to a place where we were struggling with cash flow. We questioned what we might need to change, but felt very much that we were doing what God wanted us to do. We tried extending our loan, but to no avail. We thought hard about selling part of our business but didn't feel very comfortable about that either. In amongst it all, we were praying, and seeking God for the answer. Every time it seemed that an answer would come, it would fall through. Financially, we were stretched out to the max, and everything seemed to conspire against us – I even paid our house insurance a month early, by *accident*, which pushed things harder. As I realised I had done this and that there was no way to reverse it, I felt God chuckling and saying to me *"Just watch what I can do!"* So, we kept trusting and seeking God and we kept up with our financial commitments in giving.

One morning as I was praying and seeking God for an answer for our circumstances, I had a picture of us in a boat in a wild storm *"Help, Lord, don't You care that we are about to drown!?"* The storm was rocking the boat about violently and it seemed that it would capsize. However, I felt that Jesus was saying to me, "Just hold on. Trust Me. I will rescue you soon and you will not go under." As I shared this with my husband, I felt that peace come over me again; the peace that passes all understanding, the deep peace and confidence that God would bring us through this.

It took time, though, and I learnt a new thing about stewardship.

My husband and I have both had the deep belief for most of our lives that everything we have, from possessions to finances to kids, really belongs to God and that we are simply stewards of it all. More than this, though, we also believe that we are accountable to God for what we do with all that we have, from the money that's left over, to our abilities and our time. However, these circumstances brought to my awareness another area of growth for us. Do we allow God to own our *lack*?

Sitting in a place where we couldn't even pay out the credit card (normally we wouldn't allow it to get to a point where we don't pay it off fully each month), I had to accept that we had asked God to provide for our financial needs and that we had to let go of the responsibility of the *poor stewardship* (in my mind at least) of not paying off the credit card and of having to pay interest where we hadn't planned to, as well as non-payment fees.

When I seek God to meet my financial needs, I cannot hold on to those needs, but must lay them down at His feet. While I was stressing about this, I was not resting in faith and leaving this to be His problem. I had to let go, allow this *waste*; allow God to have control of that *waste*.

I have heard the example of Mary pouring a year's salary worth of perfume over Jesus as an illustration or demonstration of how extravagant God is and how nothing is too much for Him, even as Judas was advocating how much this could have done for the poor. However, in my mind, throwing money at the bank for nothing is not a good use of resources – I would much rather give that money to someone who needed it. But, again, it was a growth in trust . Will I trust God even when things really don't look *good* or *right*, when it doesn't feel comfortable or natural? Will I make the choice to rest in Him with my finances awry and allow Him to do as He sees fit, or am I busy telling Him how to do His job?

Just as things seemed to be settling down, we had another financial hit. This time a government institution made large claims on our finances for money they hadn't claimed three years before. Even though the government had come to a place of agreeing that many of these laws had been unjust and so changed them, they had a huge backlog and were still reconciling the unjust amounts from up to seven years back. Everything in me rose up at the unfairness of *our* money being taken from us and given to someone who *we judged* not to need it.

In the midst of this, I had a husband who remained, (after the initial shock) irritatingly calm about it all, trusting in God's goodness and His promises to meet our *needs*, let alone the fact that when we look at the other two-thirds of the world, we find that we are incredibly rich by comparison. My struggle remained with the fact that if God asked us to give it all to people in need I wouldn't hesitate. It just didn't seem like good stewardship of our resources. However, I was learning that there will be times when Ie don't understand why God allows some things to happen and in true faith, I don't need to. If I really trust God, I can sit and say, "I don't understand why, but I am sure God has a reason, and I pray that it comes to fruition in His plans." We can look at situations like these and see it as being all about spiritual warfare, that the satan (the accuser[2]) is attacking us. I have no doubt that this can be so, that he has a finger in the pie, just as he did with Job. The only thing that is really important, though, is our response.

As I sought God to help me change my attitude, I felt Him showing me that the distribution of this money in such an unjust

---

[2] Many people are not aware that the term "satan" is actually a Hebrew word, which is not a name but descriptor, meaning the accuser.

fashion was part of His plan for those who received it, that it was a challenge to them to see His provision and that He was using it to bless them with the aim to draw them to Himself. However, they were only responsible to Him about their response to this, not to us. There is a level at which this was a test for us:

> *"If I take your money and give it to a person you have difficulties with and they subsequently spend it counter to what it was intended for, how will you respond? Will you be bitter and resentful, either to Me or to that person? Or will you submit to Me and continue to trust Me, even in this?"*

In the area of my possessions and wealth, or even lack thereof, I find I have a fine line to walk. I can so easily slip into a place of measuring God's love for me by what I have (or don't). I know it. I have spent many years with a deep belief — although not one I would readily have admitted even to myself — that my lack in any area was because God did not love me that much. This was an area of deep bondage in my life, which came out of rejection issues and it led to a performance orientation in me. I had to perform for God to love me and if I didn't feel that love it was because I hadn't performed.

Falling into the trap of working harder is an ongoing danger. Believing that some action of mine can make God do something for me is a subtle temptation. Even praying about situations can cause me problems. For example, if I had any belief, when praying about my finances like "If I pray, God will fix this", then I could have the wrong motivation. My motivation needs to be around seeking God, about having relationship with Him. Presenting my need before Him in the form, "God, I am struggling financially. Could You help me? What do you want me to do? What do You want to do here? What do you want to show me?" is different to saying, "God, I need more money."

It reminds me of conversations I had with my daughter when she was young. Sometimes she would get angry and frustrated because I was not helping her. I would point out to her that yelling, "My hair won't go right!" or "I can't do this!" was not asking for help. We might not be so overt with God, but we do need to come humbly to Him and in submission. It is a fine line between coming in expectation that God cares and wants to meet my needs and then expecting something specific that, although it may be in line with my desires, is not in line with His.

Coming back to where I started, there is a fairly constant reminder to me that many of the issues we feel challenged by are very much *first world* problems, problems that millions in the world would hardly flinch at, or would even wish they had the luxury of having. Perspective is a real game changer in what we struggle with, even though we often don't see it at the time.

In more recent times, my view of God confronted my understanding of Him as my Provider further. It came as I was reading through Psalms. As I got to Psalm 23, I released my my familiarity with it, and asked the Lord to show me a fresh revelation. I was using the Complete Jewish Bible, which has some significant differences and I didn't get past the first verse that day:

"*Adonai [the Lord] is my Shepherd. I lack nothing.*"

In a similar manner to the lesson with my finances, when He showed me that He was taking responsibility even for my debt, I felt Him asking me to release to Him even those areas in my life where I sensed lack. If I lack nothing, then I must have all I need. Therefore, any area where I am feeling lack is an area where

I need His change of perspective to see this area as He does. I don't have the luxury to believe that He is holding out on me, that He is not actually good, or even that He is not able. Again, this is not something that changes over night, but is a day by day walk with Him as He shifts and adjusts my sight until it lines up better with His. Beginning to wear glasses lately and finding that I have quite a strong astigmatism has given me a greater awareness of the distorting effect we can have if our vision is not 20/20. Our walk with God is a journey of continually having our vision corrected to see more clearly through His eyes.

Questions for further reflection and action

1. What instances of God's provision for you can you recall? These may range from the ordinary to the supernatural. Give Him thanks for these.

2. In what ways or aspects of your life do you think God may be challenging you to extend your trust of Him as your Provider? Is there something He wants you to let go of, or to lay down so that He can prove Himself trustworthy?

3. Are there areas in your life where you are experiencing lack? Are you ready to hand them over to God to allow Him to take care of them?

4. Spend some time meditating on the scriptures at the beginning of this chapter. What does God want to say to you through them?

Handing Back Control of Others

"You, my brothers and sisters, were called to be free. But do not use your freedom to indulge the flesh; rather, serve one another humbly in love." Galatians 5:13
"Be completely humble and gentle; be patient, bearing with one another in love." Ephesians 4:2
"Finally, all of you, be like-minded, be sympathetic, love one another, be compassionate and humble." 1 Peter 3:8

When I was in my early twenties, my mother came across an old reel-to-reel tape voice recording that my younger brothers and I had made when I was about eight or nine. We had really enjoyed the wonderful technology of recording our voices and hearing them back. This particular recording was a *radio station* segment we'd made. Listening to it was quite embarrassing for me. I couldn't believe the bossiness in my voice as I instructed my youngest brother (probably about three or four at the time) to "just say something". I had never thought of myself as being that controlling or manipulative and here it was, right out in the open!

Most of us have probably been aware of feeling as though someone else is trying to control either our lives or aspects of our behaviour at some point in our lives. Many of us would relate to this particularly in the process of breaking away from our parents. And, in all likelihood, we have each struggled with the desire to control others or their behaviour at least at some point in time. I would suggest, however, that much of our desire to control others and our relationships with them has its roots in either of two causes. The first, our desire for the best for them, can easily become tangled with the second, which is the way our brokenness manifests; our belief that our way is the only *right way*.

Having a child has been a huge growth for me in this area. Initially this was in realising just how much I desired to control the world around me. Having stepchildren stretched me even further. The truth is that as much as we would all like to control those we are in relationship with, we can't. The question becomes, then, *how do we deal with others and what we can do when they do things we would rather they didn't?*

About three weeks into parenting, I started to realise that I wasn't going to be able to make my daughter the child I wanted her to be. Although it may sound funny, I went into parenting *knowing* that I was going to be the best parent ever. I was going to deal with my child perfectly and consequently there were no problems that I (and some book) couldn't overcome. Quickly! Hmm…was I in for an eye-opening!

It started with the fact that there were times when I wanted her to be awake (for example, feed times in the day) and it seemed nothing could keep her awake. On the flip side, there were times when she was going to be awake (time to play!) and I wanted her to be asleep. Desperately. It was four am! This was already the beginning of letting go for me and I really wasn't prepared for it.

Another confrontation to my idealism arose as someone told me that I would make mistakes as a parent. After three months, I was still convinced I was invincible…or something! They told me of a book called "*Good Enough Parenting*" and explained the idea that it wasn't whether or not you made mistakes as a parent (because I would) but the overall, consistent messages that were important. I struggled to accept it at that point, but over the years it has stuck in my memory and I have learnt to be a little more lenient with myself.

If I needed further clarification of my position as a parent out of control, it came by the time my daughter was eighteen months old. She was determined and decisive and knew exactly what she wanted (or didn't), especially when it came to clothes. One of the books I had read suggested that I choose my battles carefully. That is, to only stand my ground on the issues that I saw as vitally important (for example, health and safety) and to learn to give ground on those things that are really only preference. (Thongs and shorts are fine in winter…hmmm…). Parenting has definitely been (and continues to be) a journey demonstrating just how little I can control others, however good my intentions may be.

I do recognise that most of what parents require of their children does come out of a desire for the best for them. We want kids to grow up well adjusted, confident, healthy and able to function well in society, while also being able to achieve all God created them to achieve and to have a great relationship with Him. It spells trouble if they see this end occurring through a different path than we think we see so clearly for them. It may come from our own experiences: "don't do that because I did and it had a bad outcome", or "do this because it worked for me". Unfortunately, I have to continually remind myself that as much as I might see similarities between my child and myself, she is different and God does have at least somewhat different plans for her. Even though I was determined I wouldn't pressure my daughter the way I had felt my father pressure me about the subjects she should study when she had the choice, I found myself in an internal battle again as she stepped away from certain subjects in her final year. As I reflected on how little use these subjects had been to me in the course of my life over the ensuing decades, I realised afresh that my perceptions of what I thought the world thought was important were controlling me. It was another moment of letting go — so freeing!

Reflecting further on our desires to control others, I love a story I heard where someone was complaining to God about her husband and kids and asking why He hadn't changed them. His response was along the lines of, "I want to but I am waiting for you to get out of the way." Over time, I have come to recognise the truth of how much time I have spent trying to change other people. And the further eye-opening truth is the reality that the times people actually change *through all my striving* are few and far between.

One of the first self-help books I read discussed the fact that we cannot change other people; that change is their choice. We can offer to help or give advice, but in the end, it is down to them what they do with it. The only thing we can change is the way we respond to them. In fact, our greatest power is in our own response. It is an area I am still doing a great deal of growing in and probably will for the rest of my life. It is one thing to stop responding negatively. It is a whole other lesson to learn healthy new ways to deal with our problems with others. It is probably as varied as people are and the outcome from this change is not always the outcome we would choose.

In my first marriage, I started to put some of these principles to work. We had been having our struggles. However, as I tried to bring us through to a healthier place by endeavouring to get my husband to engage with what I felt might be helpful activities with me, I came to a place where I realised that he wasn't ready to do that. If I wasn't happy with the way things were in our relationship, the only change I could make was to me.

My first step was learning to love him unconditionally. I remember doing an activity on forgiveness where I was to write him a letter stating that I forgave him for things he had done that I had felt hurt by. It wasn't to give to him, but an exercise of writing out (and reading out loud) the statement of forgiveness over and over, which took me on a process of working it through. It was much harder than I expected, however when I had finished, I felt all my love for him return in quite a rush. I suddenly began to see myself as he did, too. So I began to change. I began to stop trying to manipulate our relationship to make it work. It meant that I stopped doing some things that I did just because I felt he expected me to. On the other side, I also allowed him to do things his way, although this didn't mean I had to follow suit.

Although this freed me up quite a lot and I started to feel more peace, unfortunately it was soon after this that he decided that he didn't like the change he saw in me. In his own words, he could see that it was good for me, but he wanted me back the way I was. I learnt another hard lesson here. Even though I might change for the better, I had to accept that others may not be prepared to adapt to that change and the end result may be that the relationship can't work. (Please note, this is not the only reason our marriage ended – it was more complicated than that. However, I believe it is no coincidence that the end came only months after this. It takes two to make a relationship work.)

After the end of my first marriage, it took me some time to be prepared to even consider another relationship. When I did get to this place, I decided that I would make sure that I was the emotionally healthiest I could be before I would marry again. Although this evolved from the thought that if I was healthy, I would hopefully be able recognise unhealthy relationships, there was also a realisation (somewhere there!) that some ways I had been operating in my life were not particularly helpful when the rubber hit the road.

I went for a fair bit of counselling and at one point the counsellor confronted me with the fact that I had been living in a place where I was overly dependent on one person (my husband) to meet all my needs. At the time I understood the need for a wider circle of friends to rely on, however it was not until years later that I uncovered and dealt with the reason I had ended up in this place. It had been a conscious decision and it had to do with rejection.

Looking back into my childhood and teen years, I can pinpoint a number of incidences that led me to a position where I decided that people were basically untrustworthy. There were certain people I would trust to a deeper level, but I had developed a belief that even those people didn't really like me that much and at best were tolerating me. Because of this, I lived in a carefully constructed and controlled environment where I was very selective about who I really let in. None of this was conscious, but it was a lie that I lived with for so long and believed so deeply that it coloured my whole life. Meeting someone who put me up on a pedestal and made me the centre of his life completed the picture. I didn't need anyone else. I could survive anything if I had that relationship. *Except losing it!*

The point is, in my brokenness, I tried to fix my life through a relationship. Being married made me okay and it meant that I was making my dream happen. However, having relationships largely to meet my needs ends up being manipulative or unsatisfactory at best, especially given that only God can meet most of the needs I was looking to others to meet.

During my healing process I learnt that our basic needs include acceptance, value and belonging. We tend to look to others to *make* us feel accepted, valued and as though we belong. The problem is that no one else is perfect, and so what they reflect back to us often becomes distorted to some degree (or we distort it on the way in) and so we end up feeling cheated or let down. The only Person who can reflect our true value, who accepts us unconditionally, and who we can really belong to, is the One who created us. It is only in God that we find these needs perfectly met.

For me, though, there was another difficulty getting these needs met.

There was a point in my journey where I saw a picture of myself as a bucket. Here I was, trying to get my bucket full through healthy relationships, but I suddenly became aware that my bucket had colossal holes in it. I felt as though it wouldn't matter how much anyone poured into my bucket it would never be full as it simply flowed away through the holes. I did not have the capacity to hold what they gave me. I was quite devastated by this picture, (even though I felt no judgement from God about it), and felt I must literally be such a drain on other people, as well, constantly looking for reassurance and validation. However, as I continued, I realised that the problem wasn't just those holes, but was also a wall that I had built.

During the period of my late teens and even into adulthood, I had developed a very efficient way to not allow others to hurt me. I had built a wall. Whenever someone would do or say something that hurt me or I didn't like, another brick went up. "It doesn't matter, you're not that important to me." "You are just so and so, or such and such. What would you know?" I had a whole retinue of excuses and reasons as defences against the pricks and prods around me and over time, they built a very effective wall.

The issue is that although walls are good at keeping the bad out, they also tend to keep the good out. When someone gave me praise or love, the same thoughts would appear… "You are not important enough for that to make me any good..." "You're just saying that… If you really knew me…" Although they weren't conscious thoughts, they were there in the background, forming the foundation of how I lived.

Along my healing journey, I became aware of other various aspects of my self-protection. However, as helpful as they were in increasing my understanding of where I was and why, they did not fix the problem.

I remember a discussion where I said to someone that my belief that other people would hurt me was true. Other people are imperfect and they do hurt people. The response was a totally new thought for me. "Yes, but most people are not trying to. Most people are not vindictive and spiteful. If they hurt you, it is usually unintentional." It took me some time to take this on board, but it enabled me to take baby steps forward in having a much more forgiving attitude to others and to not continue to fortify my walls when I something they did hurt me.

Pulling down the walls around my heart has been quite painful and has taken time. However, God is gentle and I came to a point where I started to trust Him more. In as much as it took years to build and reinforce the walls, though, it also took time to bring them down. Along the journey, there were significant healing points.

At one time, I found myself going through a series of episodes where I sensed God put His finger onto an emotional wound and say, "I want to deal with that one." At first, I would try to ignore it, but I eventually realised it only meant I sat in pain for longer. As much as I would find myself crying out, "Nooooo… I don't want to go there", I became aware that accepting where I was and dealing with it, with God, was nowhere near as painful as I expected. And it was certainly less painful than what I experienced while not dealing with it.

It was in one such episode that I found myself in oceans of tears yet again in church. Sighing, I said to God, "OK, let's get on with it. What do You want me to deal with this time?" Immediately, I had a picture of a staircase going deep down into a basement, with a small door in the dark at the bottom. God was carrying a lamp and pointing His finger said, "I want to go in there."

Instantly, nearly every part of my being rose up in terror and tension and screamed out (inside me), "NOOOOO. No way. We are not going in there…" I was a mess, even though I had absolutely no idea what was behind that door. (It shows how deceptive our hearts are! See Jeremiah 17:9) However, I had learnt to trust God more, so by the morning, when I woke up still struggling, I found a miniscule amount of strength somewhere in my depths to be able to give my assent to Him, to say, "OK, show me what it is."

As I had found with most things, it was nowhere near as bad as the intensity of my feelings would have suggested. On this occasion, it was a vow I had made when my marriage had ended that caused the offending wound. "*I will never let anyone hurt me like this again.*"

Although it sounds fairly innocuous and harmless, and even sensible, in some ways this vow was the mortar that had held my wall together, perhaps even put a concrete coat over it. While the statement was about self-protection, what it actually did was prevent me from trusting others and believing them. By this time, I was remarried and it was particularly affecting our relationship. My inability to receive love at a deep level from my husband as well as the impact on my relationship with God left me quite hollow inside.

So how was I to fix this? It was a process I had been learning for some time, and rather than acting on my feelings, I needed to engage my will. I got together with a trusted pastor, we prayed over it, I renounced the words I had spoken over myself, asked God for forgiveness for making the vow and I moved on. Although incidents like this did not generally give me an instantaneous change, over a period of time I realised that I was not responding the way I had before. Other people's actions were no longer affecting me in the same way.

What it particularly meant this time was that I started to be able to believe the good others spoke of me, started to be able to accept love and care from them and my bucket started to fill up. Looking back, I realise that this had even affected my ability to accept love from God, and so, most importantly, I could now get my bucket filled by Him. In turn, this has enabled me to have so much more energy and ability to minister truly to others. What's more, I don't feel like a bucket with a hole anymore!

The reason I share this is that the broken part of me that tries to control others is really only trying to get satisfaction, to get needs met. Often this is in distorted and perverse ways and the satisfaction from these never lasts. Like the difference between eating lollies or junk food to replace a healthy meal, we go away feeling dissatisfied. Many of us live with holes in our buckets, or perhaps try to ignore our bucket completely. We might try to fill it with many things, from giving to others, to food, to drugs, to sex or even ministry or family. The issue with all these things is that they can become addictive behaviours. They only give a short-term fix, so we keep coming back for more, never really being satisfied. However, until we discover our destitution and loss when something or someone removes these props, and it seems our world collapses around us, we often don't realise our utter reliance on them to keep us going.

The cure, as I have found it, is two-fold. The first is to get our bucket fixed. Depending on the number of holes and how big they are, this can be something of a process. As much as I hated to hear this, people have reminded me that what we spend a lifetime doing to ourselves or having done to us, generally doesn't take a minute to fix. Although I do believe God can work miracles, the process is often part of the cure — we need to learn certain things along our healing journey to prevent us going back and repeating the damage.

The second part of the cure is to seek to fill our bucket from the only Source that will truly satisfy us. Our Creator. God created us for relationship, first with Him, then with others. He is the Source of all we need and it is only as we seek to live our lives in complete dependence on Him that we will not only be truly satisfied, but also fulfil all He created us to be in our relationships with others. It is only then that we have enough to give to others in their need – the times He asks us to be His hands, feet or voice.

Ultimately, we will continue to have problems for as long as we expect or desire other people to either fix us or make our lives better. God did not create anyone to do that, to be our answer. Only God is. Unless we look to Him, we will always get to a point where we are stuck. Other people will inevitably let us down, especially if we are looking to them to do something for us that God didn't design them for. As long as we keep trying to get our needs met by others in inappropriate ways, we will continue to try to manipulate and control them, endeavouring to get them to do something for us.

The same goes for us as we help others. We cannot fix other people's problems for them. We cannot fix the world. We can, and must, only point them to Jesus who both has and is the answer.

Another area I have learnt my need to release others is through forgiveness. When I hold on to unforgiveness, there is a part of me that believes the other owes me something. This, in itself, is a form of manipulation and control. If I withhold forgiveness, often I am actually trying to force you to change or do something I want. However, I will explore the impact this has had in my life further on in chapter five.

Questions for further reflection and action

1. Are there areas of your life where the desire to control others impacts relationships around you?

2. Can you identify the fear or other driver that prevents you from letting go of the outcomes in these circumstances? Pray and ask the Holy Spirit to help you to let go of these areas and to give you the strength to trust Him with these people.

3. Ask Holy Spirit to reveal to you if there is anyone you need to forgive.

4. Spend some time meditating on the scriptures at the beginning of this chapter. What does God want to say to you through them?

Handing Back Control of My Future

"For I know the plans I have for you," declares the Lord, "plans to prosper you and not to harm you, plans to give you hope and a future." Jeremiah 29:11

"That's it! I can't take it anymore!"

As my husband stormed furiously into the house from work in the middle of the day, I felt my world start to crumble around me. In shock and disbelief, I helped him find somewhere else to live, not believing that it would be for long. We would work it out. It was not that I thought we had a perfect marriage. There had been struggles for some time. It was just that I was in this for better or worse and I thought he was too. *There was something I could do to fix this.*

Over the next weeks and months, it was probably this belief that helped me survive, but it was a false belief. And I only just survived, sometimes barely.

Growing into adulthood it had taken me some time to come to a place where I realised not only that my life was mine to make of it what I wished but that it was also my responsibility. Finding out who I am and what my gifts are has been a whole other journey, which seems to have brought me in something of a full circle. In discovering the freedom of early adulthood, though, I was happy to cruise and enjoy life without much of a plan. I didn't have awareness of particular abilities nor of specific desires for my future.

A fairly unconscious assumption I had of the picture of my life included a husband I would grow old with, children and eventually grandchildren. If you had asked me, I would not have been able to verbalise this even though deep down I discounted the possibility of it not coming to pass. I had seen it in my parents' life and it is a fairly common scenario in the society I live in. There was never any sense of impending doom, or thoughts that I couldn't work through any impediments to build the life I wanted. *I could make it happen.*

In many ways, I drifted along where life took me, feeling at some levels that my choices were somehow limited, that I was somewhat boxed in. There was no question, for example, of whether I would go on to tertiary education. The choice was only what course and where, although the subjects I had taken created some limits around this, (again without seeing alternative choices), as did my scores in those subjects. Not seeing other possibilities around living arrangements, where I could travel to and from home each day also hemmed me in. Looking back, there were many alternatives, but my lack of experience and confidence formed restrictions so I struggled to break out of the expectations I perceived from others, particularly my parents, and my belief systems about what they expected of me.

And so I drifted on.

An attribute of mine I have not always valued and others have categorically not always appreciated is my ability to organise. Looking back on my childhood, I often included people in this. My two younger brothers were probably the greatest victims while they were still smaller than me and looked up to me. At one level, this is not a bad thing. People need leadership at least at some points in their lives. And for me, especially as I moved toward adulthood, it was not particularly manipulative either. I wasn't generally trying to make people do what I wanted specifically. It was simply a matter of expediency. If we are going to do this thing, let's get on with it. A case where this came to the fore was in my mid-teens, when a friend's father gave a group of girls from my school some work in the holidays to help with a large mailout. The secretary put envelopes, letters, address stickers and stamps on the table, told us what she required and left us to it. Very promptly, I realised that if each person did one task, either folding, putting on stickers or placing the letter in the envelope, we'd get the job done more quickly. We completed a job they had presumed would take us a couple of days in less than one. Hopefully none of the others realised that my organisational ability had done them out of a significant amount of pay! I did get a lovely letter of recommendation from my friend's father, though.

In my early twenties, however, I began to see that this trait could be somewhat overpowering to others. I would find myself jumping ahead, or jumping in first to get things happening in a way that did not allow others to have their input or to use their gifts. I had to learn to step back and wait for others first. In cases where it was my role to lead, I also needed to listen.

Over the course of my healing journey, I have discovered that part of this comes from a fear of things being out of control. If I organise it, I know I can rely on myself and I don't have to rely on someone else who might let me down or disappoint me. I know it will *get done right*. This included my life. Unfortunately, this also led me to a place where I didn't really trust many other people. By the time I was married, the reality of this played out as an over-emphasis on the importance of my relationship with my husband. I was still learning how to have a healthy independence from my parents, but I was so insecure within myself that deep down I found it very difficult to believe that it was ok or safe to depend on others. As I mentioned earlier, I felt that if there was one person I could rely on one hundred percent, that would make me safe.

Several things happened in the process of having a child that have retrospectively shown me the journey God has been taking me on, revealing the rather nasty fact that I cannot control the outcome of my life. Try as I might, I cannot produce the *perfect life*.

In typical naivety, we planned our family. We decided the earliest time we would like to have a baby and started from there. I did not worry or think about not conceiving, although I didn't expect immediate results. However, as pregnancy became a realistic possibility, I started to wonder if I was really ready and were there not some other things I might like to do before parenting tied us down? By the time I had those thoughts, it was too late. We were expecting.

Well, I enjoyed pregnancy and was fortunate that things were fairly normal for the first two trimesters. However, when I had my intensive thirty-week check-up, to my complete shock and surprise, the obstetrician told me I had gestational diabetes. How could this be? I was having the perfect pregnancy; I was eating and doing all the right things. I was taking control over my birthing (in a birthing unit with only midwives if I had my way), but suddenly I found myself in a place where others took certain decisions out of my hands. Such was my level of denial that one day the dietician had to tell me straight out, "You have to accept the fact that you are not having a normal pregnancy, that you are now at a higher level of risk." (One of those, I found out, being a much greater risk of placental failure and even loss of the baby.)

Even after all this and the obstetrician telling us they would induce the baby at thirty-nine weeks, I felt confident I could make myself go into labour spontaneously before then and still have my baby naturally. It did not happen. Unfortunately, because of my denial combined with a fairly full-on birthing experience (just shy of a caesarean after some thirty-plus hours of labour), I really struggled for the first few months.

And so, my baby was born. Well, I had read up heaps while pregnant. As I mentioned earlier, I was going to be a perfect parent, my baby the perfect baby. I had all the plans and I would make it happen. I remember early on, as I was doing an early morning feed, having a discussion with myself. The unrelenting responsibility of parenting had hit me like a ton of bricks and I was realising that my life was no longer my own, that the responsibility was 24/7. The discussion went something like this: "I can't keep going on like this. It is too much…" (whine). "But this is what you wanted. You went into it with your eyes open. What did you expect?"

It was at this point I relaxed with it, with my expectations on myself. As some wise sage said, and which I took on as my sanity line, "Remember, it's not forever. They do grow out of it. It's just a phase." Mind you, no one mentioned the fact that they then go into another phase that is bound to challenge you in a whole new way! The lesson I had begun some years ago on understanding that I cannot control someone else's behaviour, only my reaction to them, had just moved up a notch.

Over time, things settled down and I was back in control again. My baby finally adjusted to life outside the womb and relaxed into a very set routine. I thought life was going well as we bought a house, I headed back to university and everything was fairly predictable…

…Until the day my husband decided to leave.

As I mentioned earlier, I truly believed that I could do something to fix our marriage. I had been through a process of suggesting we have some counselling, to finding books we could use to self-help our marriage, to finally doing my bit to make sure I was not part of the problem, dealing with my own resentment and unhealthy ways of dealing with conflict.

However, a marriage takes two to make it work. If one half moves away emotionally and makes connections elsewhere, it becomes difficult if not impossible to make it work. So, I was in another place where I had no control over the events of my life. As I watched so much of what I held dear slip away, I fell into a deep black hole of despair. It took me some time to realise it, but the loss of the relationship was small compared to what felt like the loss of my whole future, the unspoken dream of how my life should turn out.

This was not something that was a once off grief incident, either. As time went on, there were constant little reminders: people celebrating 50th, 60th wedding anniversaries, the birth of the children of friends and family, birthdays and so on. All these helped to highlight the fact that even if I were to remarry and have more children and so forth, it would never quite be the same as if my marriage had lasted. It hit me hard, and was probably a major factor in my heading down that dark tunnel of despair to depression. In fact, a sense of powerlessness and lack of control is probably a leading cause in depression, so it was hardly surprising.

Looking back a number of years later, I found myself wondering about my faith at that time. As I watched someone else go through a similar experience with every appearance of a great deal more composure and strength than I had felt, I asked God what was different about my faith in that place. The picture He gave me was a little confronting. The concept that went with it was taking a small child to learn to swim. We hold them in our arms and instruct them to lie back and float, but they cling to us fearfully instead. This was the picture God gave me of myself at that time. Rather than really trusting Him through this process, I was clinging to Him, screaming and crying, "Don't let me drown." A long time later, I realised that any drowning was in more my perspective rather than actual reality. This may sound harsh, but I do believe that how we deal with the issues in our lives is far more important than what they are.

Letting go of my future has been a long journey. I am still on it, although I am getting better at recognising when I attempt to manipulate or create outcomes; I am getting better at leaving those desires with God. Although I have grown in my ability to seek God's way forward, in many cases I have continued to set them in my paradigm of what I would like rather than truly allowing God to have His way. In His mercy, God has been and continues to be gracious.

Nevertheless, I have become more and more aware of just how much I like to create parameters of acceptability on the life outcomes I would like. As much as I might say that I give my life to Jesus, there have definitely been no go zones at times of what I have and haven't allowed Him to prevent or add to my life. However, I have also come to recognise that He will regularly override these, as is His right! And I have not always even been aware of those zones until the unthinkable has happened, challenging me again. "Yes, God, I trust you in all areas of my life." Then there is an issue with my health, or a loved one's health, or my marriage, or my children, or my work situation, and I find another new area where I need to learn how to trust in God and His abilities.

For me, the process of trusting God more has generally been a gradual one, in that it has occurred as healing has taken place in other areas of my life, but also as my understanding of God has grown. My understanding of what it means to trust God has helped me to step back from my unfulfilled dreams and desires, and speak out that trust. If I am trusting God with this, that He knows best what my future needs to hold, I don't need to worry about it.

As I have reflected on where some of my incorrect or unhelpful beliefs have come from, I wonder whether it has been from subtle (or even not so subtle) incorrect teaching I have taken on board. A focus on verses such as "Take delight in the LORD, and he will give you the desires of your heart" (Ps 37:4) out of context with the rest of the Bible can lead to a belief that God is all about making me happy. I wonder if the whole movement encouraging women as 'Daughters of the King' and 'Princesses' and deserving royal treatment, although helpful at many levels, may also lead people to believing that God is all about making them feel good and supplying all our wants (not needs! Phil 4:19). Again, the issue is not even necessarily the truth of the teaching, but that when it is out of balance with other instruction, it can lead to self-focus and self-fulfilment rather than a life focussed on God.

Another aspect of this for me was about having a vision for my life. Although we definitely need some sort of vision to work toward, it seems that, as with many aspects of life, it is easy to swing too far one way. I did find it really helpful to explore my spiritual gifts and look at my role in life through that lens. However, if I turn my purpose in life into being about using my spiritual gifts, it can subtly become very self-serving. I want to self-actualise and do whatever it takes to be the best, whatever that might mean. (I have a sneaking suspicion that that is all about other people's perception!) The question I keep asking myself is whether not doing a certain activity/ministry/job makes me less of a person, less valuable to God in my own eyes, or whether, conversely, doing it makes me *more*. If the answer is yes, then my motives still need some work. Rather than serving God and others, maybe I am still in a position of trying to fulfil myself and who I think I need to be.

Don't get me wrong here. Finding the ways in which God had gifted me, the way He created me, was an important part of my journey to self-love and self-acceptance. One of my big issues growing up was not knowing who I was and struggling with being someone separate to others. So much of my idea of self was based on my perceptions of how others viewed me, which often had little basis in reality. I was very good at reading great depths of understanding into every little response and act by another toward myself, or even in my vicinity. If you didn't speak to me, I could easily read it as a snub, whether or not you had actually noticed I was there. And I was equally good at reading great depths into random comments that were in all likelihood never in the mind of the speaker. Learning that God made me in a certain way, with certain abilities and gifts was important in my understanding of my purpose.

From the place of understanding that God did have a specific plan for my life, He also started to plant a vision for ministry in my heart. Connecting my gifts and abilities with this vision lead me to a place where I wanted to do everything in my power to make it happen; take every opportunity, rush ahead. However, there was also a point when I realised that although God had given me a vision, it wasn't up to me to then make that vision happen by myself.

A major understanding came through another picture. Jesus and I were standing on a mountain top, looking out across a valley. There was a town in the valley, and He pointed at the town and said, "That's where we're going." My response was, "Great, let's get going", with the idea of making a beeline for it. However, as I unpacked this picture, I realised that when you come down a mountain, you don't simply go straight down. That could lead to a lot of damage if not destruction. You have to follow the trail, which winds about and sometimes even goes around the back of the mountain, looking like it is going in the wrong direction.

The message for me from this was that I had to follow the path He was taking. This was not simply to get to the *destination*, but along the way He would teach and strengthen me, not to mention give me opportunities to touch other people's lives. This vision has very much played out over the years. I feel as though I am a lot closer to that destination, but not quite there yet. I am also a lot more ready for what it involves than when I started. I look back and know without a doubt that God's wisdom and methodology is so far above mine, and I am so glad I didn't take my own path too often.

Along the journey, there have been many other little lessons. So often I would be impatient that we weren't getting to the destination; that we seemed to be going in completely the wrong direction. I would see others getting opportunities that God (or others!) didn't open to me and I would cry out to Him, "Why is this person or that person getting to do x?", or, "why do they get noticed and I don't?" Each time, He would come back, so gently, "Whose approval are you looking for? Whose way do you want to do this – Mine or man's?" He reminded me that His logic, His methodology and His ways were different to what seemed rational or sensible in human wisdom.

At times I struggled because there were so many Christian books written about what we need to do to get where God wants us, by people who were well esteemed by other notable Christians. When I talked to God about this, I felt Him say, "This is not for you". It was at one such time of soul searching that my inbox contained an email with the following message. It confronted me to the core, as it spoke into so many of my feelings that I felt like it was a prophetic word written just for me. I was so surprised when I found it was written something like 100 years before. Mind you, it did encourage me that I was not alone in feeling this way.

Others May, You Cannot

If God has called you to be really like Jesus, He will draw you into a life of crucifixion and humility, and put upon you such demands of obedience, that you will not be able to measure yourself by other Christians; and in many ways, He will seem to let other good people do things which He will never let you do.

Other Christians and ministers, who seem very religious and useful, can push themselves, pull wires and work schemes to carry out their Christian goals, but these things you simply cannot do. Others may boast of their work or their writings or their success, but the Holy Spirit will not allow you to do any such thing, and if you ever try it, He will lead you into some deep mortification that will make you despise yourself and all your good works.

Others may be allowed to succeed in making money, but most likely God will keep you poor, because He wants you to have something far better than gold, namely, a helpless dependence on Him and the joy of seeing Him supply your needs day by day out of an unseen Treasury.

The Lord may let others be honored and keep you hidden and unappreciated because He wants to produce some choice, fragrant fruit for His coming glory, which can only be produced in the shade. He may let others do a work for Him and get the credit for it, but He will make you work on and on without others knowing how much you are doing; and then, to make your work still more precious, He may let others get the credit for the work which you have done, and thus make your reward ten times greater when Jesus comes.

The Holy Spirit will rebuke you for little words or deeds or even feelings, or for wasting your time, which other Christians never seem to be concerned about, but you must make up your mind that God is an infinite Sovereign and He has a right to do whatever He pleases with His own. He may not explain to you a thousand things which puzzle your reason in the way He deals with you, but if you will just submit yourself to Him in all things, He will wrap you up in a jealous love and bestow upon you many blessings which come only to those who are very near to His heart.

Settle it then, that He is to have the privilege of tying your tongue, or chaining your hand, or closing your eyes, in ways that He does not seem to use with others. Now, when you are so possessed with the living God that your secret heart becomes pleased and delighted with this peculiar, personal, private, jealous guardianship and management of the Holy Spirit over your life, then you will have entered the very vestibule of heaven itself.

G. D. Watson (1845-1924)

Part of the lesson I was learning here was that we cannot dictate to God the order of the lessons, or even which ones we would like to learn. Submitting to Him means giving up my *rights* and even the dreams that I believe He has given me. Anything I am holding onto too tightly is fair game to God – my experience is that it is often these things that He puts His finger on to say, "Will you let Me have this?" When I feel resistance to an immediate, "Yes, Lord!", it is a warning to me to check my motivations and my heart.

And there were plenty of times where I did battle over this. After some deep healing, I was raring to get on with some ministry. I was looking for whatever opportunities I could find to prove to others what I believed God had placed in me, that I could do this. One such opportunity was a short term ministry trip we went on to Russia and the Ukraine. Much of this was being involved in a teaching team, and we were all to be prepared to speak to various groups as we went along.

At one point, I was beginning to struggle again, feeling as though the leader gave everyone else far more opportunities to speak than me. I vividly remember the chat I had with God in the back of a taxi one evening, as we headed back to our accommodation in downtown Perm. As per usual, my questions came back more as a complaint than a true question!

"When is it going to be my turn, Jesus?" Immediately I had a picture of His throne room. Jesus was sitting on His throne, and people were coming in and out. They would come up to the throne, and Jesus would hand them a scroll and they would head out to follow their instructions. I was standing to one side of His throne, trying to step in front to receive my scroll or otherwise get His attention in case He had forgotten me, but it seemed that it was never my turn. Someone else was always there first. I finally asked Jesus when He was going to give me a scroll, and He looked me full in the face in that so loving way He has, and said, "Isn't it enough for you to just be with Me?" Ouch. If I am truly honest, that is a question I still grapple with at times.

Around this time, another message I heard further confronted me about this issue. The message was about pottery vessels used in Biblical times, particularly around the idea that a potter would make a large variety of vessels, most having ordinary, everyday uses. However, every now and then the potter would make one with a special purpose, for a special client. He kept these vessels out the back in a special storage room, waiting for the right customer. What was interesting about these vessels was that the potter chose them for the customer, rather than the customer choosing the vessel they wanted. When a particular customer came in looking for a special vessel, the potter would know exactly the vessel that was for them and go out to retrieve it from its waiting place on the shelf out the back.

The part of this message that particularly struck me was when he switched the story from being about the Potter to the view the pottery had. The explanation was that we were the vessels and God is the Potter. The scenario the speaker described seemed to point directly at me.

He suggested that some of us felt like we had been sitting in that storeroom waiting to be chosen for a very long time. Every time the Potter came in, we felt hope rise. Surely this time He must pick me... But no, it was someone else, again. Finally, the day comes when the Potter comes in again, and this time, He is heading straight towards me, He is coming my way, His hand is reaching out toward me…hooray, He is going to pick me…but no! He has picked the vessel next to me.

The message went on that while I continue to respond from a position of self, from a position of *my turn*, I am still not ready. Until I am prepared to let God do the choosing in His time, and my only focus is on simply being, rather than doing, I am probably not ready. Unfortunately, I think we can go off hastily and unready at times, and although God will often use us even so, there are many examples where we do as much damage as good from this position.

Waiting, on the other hand, seems like such as waste, when I feel I could be doing so much more for the Kingdom. It is a question I still don't have all the answers to, but do know that there are certain things I cannot do now, because the level of spiritual discomfort I feel precludes me. I know without a doubt that it is not a path God wants me to go down. Of course, I can push through that, or ignore my feelings, but experience and observation has taught me it is really not worth it. A somewhat humorous example was a period of time where I decided I would apply for a paid position.

As I went through the process, not only did I not receive any offers, often I did not even get a response at all. In conversation with the Lord at one point, I said to Him, "What is going on? Not even an interview?" In the past, I had never had any problems getting a job. The very next application, I was very surprised to get a telephone call asking me to come in for an interview. However, although I tried hard to want the position, by the time I had finished the interview, I knew without doubt the job was not for me even if they had offered it to me. I felt Jesus' amusement in it all, "there you go, have an interview, are you happy now?" It cemented for me, however, that regular employment working for any boss (except Him) was not for me.

One of those annoying things my husband kept saying to me, (annoying because I know it is true), as I struggled through this phase was, "Enjoy the journey." Often, my focus has been so set on the destination that the journey has seemed a *necessary evil*. Disturbingly, I realised that living life that way, I actually discounted so much that was going on around, in, and through me as side show or as simply incidental. I have since come to an understanding that first, nothing is a loss in God's economy if I partner with Him in what He is doing, and second, there is no plan B, it is all part of plan A, and third, nothing is incidental: everything that happens to us and around us has potential to be part of plan A.

In so many ways, the future has become a lot more irrelevant to me. In one sense, every moment is the future and those moments seem to come at ever increasing speed. In another sense, rather than living in fear of missing out on my future because I have taken a wrong step, or missed an opportunity, I now realise that God is not so mean spirited or tricky. He doesn't give us one opportunity to get it right. If we centre our hearts and motivations on Him, He will guide us. In as much as I must lay down my desires and expectations of life, I must also trust the fact that He has promised to give me His Spirit, and that His Spirit dwells in me. I can trust Him to make me very uncomfortable if I stray too far off The Way, especially if I am overtly asking Him to guide me.

Part of my problem is that I forget this at times and start thinking I am not hearing from Him. So, I try to leave the future to Him, allowing Him to prompt me as He will when there are big shifts ahead, and seeking to trust that Still Small Voice in the every day.

Questions for further reflection and action

1. The desire to see into the future is pretty strong across many cultures. It is why "fortune tellers", reading tea leaves or astrology and so on has such an allure. How important is it to you to know what your future holds? Can you identify any fears that prevent you from giving the outcomes for your future to God?

2. If God holds your future in His hands, what might He have to say to you about that future? What would it look like for you to stop trying to control the outcomes of your future?

4. Spend some time meditating on the scriptures at the beginning of this chapter. What does God want to say to you through them?

Handing Back Control of God

"Remain in me, as I also remain in you. No branch can bear fruit by itself; it must remain in the vine. Neither can you bear fruit unless you remain in me. I am the vine; you are the branches. If you remain in me and I in you, you will bear much fruit; apart from me you can do nothing... If you remain in me and my words remain in you, ask whatever you wish, and it will be done for you. This is to my Father's glory, that you bear much fruit, showing yourselves to be my disciples. As the Father has loved me, so have I loved you. Now remain in my love. If you keep my commands, you will remain in my love, just as I have kept my Father's commands and remain in his love. I have told you this so that my joy may be in you and that your joy may be complete." John 15:4-10

The place of work in my relationship with God is one I continue to wrestle with. In many aspects, I believe it is part of the fruit of the tree of the knowledge of good and evil. So much of our human nature is set on the judgement of what is right or wrong, or morality, and we are continually making choices about which path we will take. When those paths are less about morality and seem more about personal choice, I can find myself tied up in ever increasing knots about my decision making.

As I struggle with mental gymnastics, I also find that although I can acknowledge and even experience God's unconditional love, there is a voice that continues to taunt me that I don't deserve it, and that I better keep doing the *right stuff* to keep receiving it. While I am far more aware of this battle in me these days, and can often head it off before it gets a grip on me again, it is one of those battles that I may continue to fight for some time yet.

Looking back over my journey, though, I can see that I am far ahead of my starting point. In my teens, when I first became aware of the idea of my faith being far more about a relationship with Jesus than about behaviour, so much teaching I received still reinforced that *this* was the sort of behaviour that was pleasing to God, but *that* was not, whether it be smoking, drinking, sex before marriage, women preaching or having uncovered hair, and so on. Added to this mix was my own sense of inferiority and lack of self-confidence or worth.

For me, the whole idea of a personal relationship with God had not been something I was really aware of, even though there had been stirrings of desire for that relationship for some time. I was always interested in spiritual things as a child – I remember getting the Bible Society show bag at our local show, and going to vacation Bible school in the holidays. I also remember coming home from church one Sunday when I was about nine and looking up at the sky and saying to Jesus, "If you're really real, show Yourself to me." I know I wanted Him to reveal Himself physically, just as I was looking for proof when we tried walking on water in our swimming pool, although I now recognise that He has honoured that prayer in so many other ways.

In the 1980s, when I was in my teens, the message I heard about becoming a Christian seemed to be more about escaping hell, even though the *reward* was a relationship with God. Indeed, one of my recurring nightmares was that Jesus had returned taking everyone else, but leaving me behind. My other recurring nightmare was about nuclear war ending the world, so you can imagine I was living in a good deal of fear at that time. Amidst this, one of the first overt answers to prayer I personally had was that God would stop those nightmares. At the point where I was getting scared of going to sleep because of the prevalence of these sorts of dreams, I prayed, asking Him to stop them and He did so immediately. I never had another.

However, this was also a reflection of my prayer life at this point. My understanding of my relationship with God was very much about me doing the right things and in return, God would give me what I want. Even though this wasn't an overt statement either in my mind or by others, at quite a deep level, it was how I was operating. There were a few of those deals I did with Him. "Please God, don't let this happen", or "please God, make this happen" and so on.

As strange as it seems to me now, God did seem to answer many of those prayers in the way I asked. Looking back, and also observing other young (in faith) Christians, I can't help wondering if He takes us on a journey of deepening our faith in stages. At first, answering those simple, self-focussed, often desperate prayers seems that it does build our faith. If God will answer this prayer, maybe next time I will pray a bigger prayer.

As I have continued in my faith journey, though, there have been significant points where He has not answered prayers the way I would have liked. For me, this has done two things. At times, it has led me to a place where I start to doubt God's love or His goodness. More recently, it has led me to start asking God about those things, and the exciting part of that is that so often He has given me understanding that actually deepens both my faith in Him and my knowledge about who He is and how He works all things together for good.

One example that comes to mind is when we were going through drought that lasted for ten years. We live on a property without town water, and so, are reliant on rainfall to fill our tanks. When our usage exceeds our collection, we have to call and pay a water carter. There were a number of times during this season where we were buying water pretty much monthly and I was struggling with the added cost of it, as our cash flow was not great at that point, either. So often I would hold out, hoping that the promised rain would be more than promised, or that a miracle would occur. And just as often, we would get less rain, or even none at all. We even had a time where the pump failed and we lost the weeks' worth of water I was hoping would carry us to the next rainfall!

The conversation I had with God around this time went something like this: "Ok, God, I am praying for rain to fill our tanks, but it is not happening. Your word says that You promise to supply all our needs, and I would say water is a pretty basic need. What's going on?" There were a couple of things I felt Him touch my heart with at that time. One was that what He was doing was about a much bigger picture than our simple needs, that He was speaking to our state and our nation if we had ears to hear. It was also an opportunity for us to feel that pain of not having enough water, to experience what so many others in our world go through. Most clearly, though, He told me that He was supplying our needs in that we had the money and accessibility to buy the water we needed. This was an important lesson in learning more about praying in God's will and understanding as opposed to my own.

Coming to understand the order of the relationship has been a major growth area in my journey with God. That is, that God is God, and I am not. And, that it is really important to keep that order in line. I believe that one of our big issues as humans is our desire to be god, to be the one in control. And I guess that comes back to the bottom line of this book.

Why do I need to be in control, what am I trying to control, and to what ends do I want that control?

Uncovering my true beliefs and motives in regards to these questions has been an important part of my healing and my freedom.

A friend's description of her conversation with her daughter regarding *unanswered* prayer was another good illustration. She explained that God was not a puppet for us to be pulling the strings and making Him dance to our tune. It reminded me of reading Isaiah 46:1-4 at one point, when a few things suddenly became very clear to me:

> *"Bel bows down, Nebo stoops low; their idols are borne by beasts of burden. The images that are carried about are burdensome, a burden for the weary. They stoop and bow down together; unable to secure the burden they themselves go off into captivity. "Listen to Me, O house of Jacob, all you who remain of the house of Israel, you whom I have upheld since you were conceived, and have carried since your birth. Even to your old age and grey hairs I am He, I am He who will sustain you. I have made you and I will carry you; I will sustain you and I will rescue you.*

What struck me was the contrast here between idols we make and God. We have to work for an idol – it can do nothing itself. It cannot even move itself, let alone perform anything for the worshipper. It is simply a burden for those who would worship it. On the other hand, God says it is He who *created us*, *He* who *carries us*, *He* who *provides for us* and *He* who *rescues us*.

When I read this, I was also reading an historical novel which was set in pagan Ireland. The description of the pagan rites of sacrifice helped me to understand the issues of idolatry further. In the novel, the community had decided that a certain person had upset the gods because of her lack of conformity, and that was why the crops had failed. In order to make the gods happy again, they must give a life. They had decided that life must be hers.

Although we read material like this and our response is that we would never do anything like that, I realised that much of my relationship with God did come out of something of that belief system. Some of the beliefs included, "If bad stuff happens to me, or good stuff doesn't, it is because God is unhappy with me." Or, "If I don't read my Bible enough or pray enough, or do enough good works, God won't do what I want Him to." And there it is. The belief that I can manipulate or control God through my actions. This is the basis of idolatry. And this belief is really insidiously entrenched in our nature.

Around this time, God gave me another closely allied insight to this concept of idolatry, related to pride. It was one of those "aha" moments, where something suddenly became crystal clear, and as I understood it, I knew I would never forget it, either.

What Holy Spirit showed me was that all my feelings of inferiority, failing and worthlessness, and my subsequent attempts at self-improvement were actually rooted in pride rather than any sort of humility. At best, it was false humility. *There was a false belief in me that I actually had the capacity to change myself*. The reality is that if I can fix myself, Jesus died in vain. His death was a waste.

This seems quite counter-intuitive to our understanding of pride. In the Australian culture I grew up in, the concept of the *Tall Poppy Syndrome* was innately part of our thinking. (To explain, Tall Poppy Syndrome is the idea that anyone determined to be a bit full of themselves deserved to be cut down a peg or two, or maybe more.) I remember even as a five year old, seeing a boy from school who was very outspoken about his abilities falling off his bike while riding without holding the handlebars and thinking he got what he deserved. In the particular Christian environment I grew up in, I took on board an idea that I should not really think of myself at all.

Perhaps part of the problem is that we often see pride as arrogance. Dictionary definitions of pride range from explaining it as an accurate opinion of one's own worth to an exaggerated opinion of self. In amongst these definitions, I have come up with a philosophy of pride that has a corresponding theological impact. I believe that the pride talked of in the Bible, although it often refers to arrogance and an overweening sense of one's own importance or status, could quite readily be applied to most of us. The old English term for pride was vanity. It comes from the same root as the word vain. The word vain actually comes from the Latin, *vanus*, which means empty, without substance. If someone is seen as being vain, then, we could say that they have an opinion of themselves that is without substance, whether that be thinking themselves better than they really are, or less than they really are.

There came a point where God revealed some of the pride in my own life. If I only think of pride as being arrogance, I can easily overlook the outworking of pride in my life. Appearing arrogant or prideful can just as easily be a cover-up for a lack of self-esteem. Although a definition of pride is to think more of yourself than you should, when we operate in a proud way, it may well be that we actually may not think well of ourselves at all. This was the case for me.

My life experiences and personal wiring had led me to a position of believing that I should not expect others to help me, that they were far too busy, or that their problems were worse than mine, and that I should be able to sort out my own *mess*, (which actually should read *life*). Although this probably didn't come from anywhere that looked particularly insidious, insidious it became in my life. It developed into a deep-seated belief that I needed to be self-sufficient. The rather obvious flow through of self-sufficiency is that you believe that you don't (or shouldn't) need anyone, not even God.

Although the link is not necessarily apparent, God has shown me that self-sufficiency is actually very closely linked with pride. If I operate out of self-sufficiency, there is an aspect of belief that I am self-sufficient, which in turn means that I can do all things for myself. This includes making myself righteous before God. If that were true, I would have no need of a Saviour. And so the link to pride. I don't need God, and I don't need Jesus. That, to me, would seem to be thinking more of myself than I should.

This was never a conscious train of thought for me. However, it does highlight the nature of the battle we are in. We have an enemy who does not want us to be dependent on God, because he knows that when we master this, we can achieve anything (Matthew 19:26: "Jesus looked at them and said, "With man this is impossible, but with God all things are possible.""). My attachment to self-sufficiency did not suddenly appear from nowhere, but was something that quite likely was handed down through family history.

My father's parents had moved to England (from Australia) when they were newly married, and ended up staying for much of the duration of World War II. My grandfather was ministering in a church in Islington, a central district of London. Although my grandmother went to live further out with the children, they lived through the blitz daily wondering whether my grandfather was still alive. I believe that they survived this emotionally crippling time with an attitude of "just suck it up and keep going". (Although back then the label was probably the British term of "keeping a stiff upper lip".)

While there was a measure of strength in this, it may have meant that people did not talk about or overtly deal with those things which caused fear or anxiety. My grandparents were also very purposeful in helping others less fortunate. I think that at times, this may have even been at the expense of the needs of their own family. And so, the development of self-sufficiency. They taught their children to be helpful, which meant putting the needs of others before their own, and pitching in for the good of everyone.

Although it is quite apparent that this way of thinking has its roots in Christianity, there is something missing. It can seem easy and even expedient to push our feelings aside and not bother with them, but unfortunately, many times they come back to impact us at a later date, either in our physical health, our mental health or both. We need to find the balance between allowing our emotions to drive us and ignoring them completely.

Dealing with negative emotions has not been straightforward for me. The belief that many others were worse off than me and so I shouldn't look for or expect help but deal with it myself was like water to the seed of self-sufficiency, which continued to grow.

As a young pre-pubescent, these actions and attitudes of my parents and others (prevailing at the time) further reinforced my self-sufficiency. Going through healing in later years, I have realised there were so many sub-conscious choices I made growing up. I remember the first time I was on the receiving end of teasing and name calling in primary school from my supposed friends. It was a knife in my guts, and the hurt and shock of it led to distrust. Moving house soon after this found me trying to make new friends in a small school in a small community where it seemed to take a long time for people to accept you as a local, or as part of the group.

These things coloured me for a long time, and grew other seeds, too. By the end of secondary school, I had my protection well established. One of my main props was the thought that eternity would sort out who was okay and justice would prevail for the rest. Although I was not conscious of treating people badly because of this thought, it quite likely made me appear proud and superior. I think I had a bit of an attitude of *reject before you get rejected*, which impacted all my relationships.

The final straw for me came in the ending of my first marriage. The level of betrayal by someone I thought was in it with me for life, that we were a partnership and would protect each other from the pain inflicted by the world was indescribable. The rejection, although not felt as such, meant that my wall was now impregnable by anyone. It wasn't until well into my healing journey that I came to a place of understanding what I had done.

Another experience where I further realised just how little I had trusted God was at a healing service. At the end of the service, the preacher invited people to bring anything they would like healing for to Jesus.

I had been feeling as though God and I had dealt with so much. I was in a much better place than previously and wondered if there was anything more necessary. However, knowing how much more freedom I had from previous healing, I did want more if that were available. So I offered up a little prayer, not one filled with much expectation, simply asking Jesus if there was anything He wanted me to bring for healing. And immediately wished I hadn't. Well, sort of. The response I heard was, "I want you to bring Me your broken heart."

Wow! I wasn't expecting that. And I certainly wasn't expecting my own response to that request. It was so difficult for me. I had a picture of me with my heart in a beautifully lined box, and I was so protective of it. I was letting no one near it, and trusting no one with it, really. I saw all this as I heard Jesus' response to me, and it devastated me on two counts.

Firstly, although I knew I wanted to give my heart completely to Jesus, to trust Him completely with it, I was also desperately afraid to do this. There was a part of me that didn't want my heart hurt again, and believed that I was the only one who could adequately protect it. At the same time, there was a bigger and probably stronger part of me that knew Jesus as trustworthy of my heart. But it was still a painful battle. Very much a cry of, "Lord, I believe, help me in my unbelief".

The second sadness I felt was that I had fooled myself for so long that I had actually given my heart one hundred percent to Jesus. How many times had I sung songs such as "Lord, I give You my heart, I give You my soul"? And yet here I found myself with a very vivid picture, which I knew was the truth, of just how much I was protecting and hiding my heart.

That night, I spent quite some time weeping in grief, both because I struggled and because of the fact that I had fooled myself for so long. However, in the midst of this, I had such a strong picture of Jesus sitting beside me, simply being with me in that place. I think it was a cathartic time and a release, and even though I went home that night feeling raw and still not quite sure I trusted Jesus with my heart, quite astoundingly, over the next few weeks, I found myself in a new place. Slowly and inexorably change happened without me really being aware of it, until suddenly I realised, "I do trust Jesus with my heart. Actually, I wouldn't want it anywhere else but with Him."

Another part of this journey occurred through some counselling sessions I was having. I remember at one point having the discussion about my difficulty in trusting others because of the reality that people do hurt you, albeit unconsciously and without malice. If I took my wall down and let people in, what would protect from this hurt? The understanding that it was God who protected me and kept me safe emotionally, had been growing in me, but I still wasn't sure what this looked like in living life.

Quite suddenly I had a picture of myself in a giant bubble, a bit like those we like to blow with detergent and water, except this bubble represented God's love for me. It was beautiful and reflected colours and life, just like those bubbles. However, my concern was how it would not pop. Just as instantaneously, God showed me that it was very strong, and that the *fiery darts* from my enemy could not pierce it. I felt He also showed me that it was like a *selective membrane*, in that it would allow good things to pass in and out, while protecting me from the bad. As long as I remained in His love, I would be safe.

However, it is up to me to remain in the place where God's love protects me. If I step back, step away from Him, then I step out and away from His protection. It reminds me of John 15:9, *"Now remain in my love."* This is an ongoing process, just as the children of Israel had to collect manna every day, so do I need to remain in His love every day. I cannot expect to just get a top up every now and again and that be enough, even though it can be tempting at times to feel that going to a conference or reading a great book or having a great time of worship is the only way I can really feel close to God. He wants me to have that experience every day, but it is up to me to position myself to live it out.

I know that this can be a really hard thing to understand. What does it actually look like to live in the place of God's love being my protection from harm? If you have been through circumstances of great harm, it is tempting to ask where God's protection was in those circumstances. Personally, I have been through the experience of God healing some memories and transforming them completely, showing me that He was there in that place. Through this I have realised His protection and healing of my inner being in a way I would never have thought possible. To explain, I will share one such memory.

The occasion was the day my husband came home in the middle of the day to say he was leaving. He was extremely angry and was yelling at me. This was a very traumatic time, not the least in that, for me, it was completely out of the blue. I was in complete shock. This memory remained a very painful one for me for many years. Using a technique called theophostic healing, I went back into that memory, inviting Jesus to be by my side and show me where He was during that incident. As strange as it sounds, He changed it.

As I asked Jesus where He was during that incident, I suddenly saw Him in place of me. My husband was yelling at Jesus. At first this disturbed me also, but then I saw that Jesus was a bit like superman – the words were simply bouncing off Him and having no effect. When I asked where I was, I saw myself in our lounge room with the Father and Holy Spirit. My daughter had been asleep at the time, and I saw that there were two angels standing guard at her door, protecting her.

While this might seem a strange story, for me it has become far more real than the old memory. It is actually hard to remember that time and it is quite vague now, whereas before this experience, it was a vivid and strongly painful memory. In my mind, what happened is as God has since shown me, not what I thought I experienced. God has done this for a number of painful memories of mine, and I am sure He can do it for anyone else, too.

Questions for further reflection and action

1. Are there areas in your life where you are aware of your own desire to control God? What do you think might be underlying these?

2. Ask Holy Spirit to reveal any areas where idolatry is operating in your life, with the understanding that an idol is any area you wont allow God to touch in your life. Are you ready to hand them over to Him?

3. If God is ultimately in control, what role does that leave you with in your relationship with Him? What do you need to give Him?

4. Spend some time meditating on the scriptures at the beginning of this chapter. What does God want to say to you through them?

Handing Back Control of the World

"...You do not belong to the world, but I have chosen you out of the world."
John 15:19
"In this world you will have trouble. But take heart! I have overcome the world."
John 16:33b
"Do not conform to the pattern of this world, but be transformed by the renewing of your mind." Romans 12:2

There are numerous beliefs I have had (and continue to discover) that I am learning are not as true as I once thought. Many of these are truths we are taught, often only by inference and often at a subconscious level, about how the world works and about how to succeed at life and even about what is important. I continue to grapple with how I can live in the world but not be overcome by the world's way of thinking. It pervades every part of our lives, from our way of living physically, to our way of thinking and behaving. What is acceptable, what is not, how to get our needs met; all these are prescribed by the society we live in. While we may see some of these in line with our faith, others are not so helpful to us, and others yet again can be a real deterrent to faith. How do we live in our society, our culture, and yet be separate?

As a teenager, I really struggled with the verses about losing our life if we wanted to save it, and not being of the world. How could I enjoy all the promises of life if I was to be separate and different?

It seemed to me that to be a good Christian, I needed to give up everything of pleasure or enjoyment.

Part of this came from inaccurate beliefs about Christianity. As I grew in understanding, however, the issue of being in the world did not go away. It simply became more subtle.

On reflection, I am aware that much of my desire to control the world around me arose from my perception of my need for safety and security. How can I indemnify myself against loss and damage? In certain aspects, faith in God can be viewed as something of an *insurance plan*, that when all else fails, or catastrophe strikes, God is there to pick up the pieces. I have discovered that this is a limited way of thinking, and in the end has not proved out, at least not in obvious ways. God hasn't often come in and *waved the magic wand*, restoring things to their former glory. He hasn't always answered my prayers in the way I would have liked, even when I have thought they were in line with His heart and His Word.

A large portion of this chapter is an exploration of my experience of God counter to how I would like Him to be at times. It is this aspect where I resonate with the assertion in the Chronicles of Narnia that "He's not a tame lion", and the Biblical reflection that "His ways are higher than ours" (Isaiah 55:9). There are two major aspects where I have been confronted by the difference between God's way of dealing with issues and what would seem logical, or the way in which the world would tell us is the right way.

The first is my idea of justice. Closely linked with this is the counter-intuitive concept of forgiveness. Although I grew up with the idea of forgiveness as prevalent in the formation of my faith, until I experienced something I found exceptionally difficult to forgive, I really didn't understand the actual process. How do I enact forgiveness?

In my younger years, I think I believed that forgiveness just meant that I didn't say anything about the incident, let it drop so to speak, and move on. The trouble came when that was not enough, and I found that underneath I was still angry. However, because anger was a very scary emotion to me growing up, I was good at suppressing it to the point where I wasn't even aware of being angry, particularly in relationships where I didn't feel confident.

When I learnt a bit more about forgiveness, I started to get a better handle on the reality of my lack of forgiving in certain circumstances. Two things stood out at one point. The first was realising that forgiveness was not a feeling, but an act of my will. That is, I needed to decide to forgive even when I didn't feel like it.

The second point was closely linked to this; that forgiving meant letting go of my *right* to justice, to paying back hurt for hurt. This second idea really helped me because I now know that if I am still feeling that desire to hurt or even see the other party hurt, it is a good indicator that I haven't completely forgiven them.

None of this makes forgiveness easy. Injustice is a strong driver for me. Seeing people get away with behaviour that causes hurt or loss to others, especially innocent others, is something that arouses a good deal of passion in me. Determining which causes I personally need to advocate for is a continuing journey.

Returning to the link between injustice and forgiveness, a further dimension arises from the emotional impact of fear. In fact, I have discovered that much of my railing against injustice in my own life, and struggle with forgiveness is undergirded by fear. As I have described in much of this book, my fear has often been related to feeling a lack of value or of belonging, almost to the point of wondering if my existence has any purpose or meaning.

My fear of my own inadequacy and the belief that there were aspects of my person and personality that were basically unacceptable to others tainted my relationships for a long time. Because of this position or belief, I either withdrew from others or tried to bring them down to my level. I know that I am far from alone in this type of behaviour although I am equally sure many people do not actually recognise that this is how they live. But it is a place of bondage.

Trying to get my needs met through acknowledgement, recognition and approval from others has proved unsatisfactory at least, if not completely inadequate. It was never enough, so always led to seeking more, like an addict looking for the next fix. It has only been as I have experienced the complete acceptance and unconditional love that God offers me that I have been able to move on from this desire. It is from this place that it has become a great deal easier to truly forgive others and cease trying to make them see the *error of their ways*. It is from this place that I feel far freer to offer unconditional love and acceptance to others.

This brings me back to my desire to control the world around me (and beyond). When I was no longer acting from a place of fear (mostly fear of loss of self), and seeking justice for myself, many of the things that used to really bother me suddenly lost their power. Circumstances which had previously had my thoughts stewing around and around no longer had that affect. I experienced so much more freedom in my mind and in my being.

However, injustice and forgiveness are not the only interactions with the world that cause us problems. I believe that the biggest battle we have is in our thinking and our true beliefs which are not always just what we think we believe or state we believe. Romans 12:2 reminds us, "Do not conform any longer to the pattern of this world, but be transformed by the renewing of your mind."

Much has been written about this, and even science is realising that the truth is that our minds and even some of our DNA can be formed and changed by the way we think. Change is possible. Personally though, I don't think we can accomplish a complete positive change on our own. We need the help of God.

As I have shared in previous chapters, letting God have control of various aspects of my life has been a journey of change and of healing. As I have continued with this, I have realised that there is always more than I expected. I see and understand aspects of myself and the world and the interaction of the two that I never even knew existed. What I have thought important and even essential, I have come to learn is often neither, and I have gained a greater depth of understanding about some concepts that I had failed to understand the relevance of previously.

One such area is the story of humankind. We are given a description from science that at best ignores the relationship of people and our planet to God. Growing up with a background in science, as well as studying science at a tertiary level, I love to understand how things work. This curiosity has also been integral to my faith journey. So often, I have found it difficult to understand or truly accept certain doctrine because I couldn't understand how or why it was important. I suppose in many ways, I have never been one for adhering blindly, or giving only superficial assent to my beliefs.

There were a couple of occasions where God challenged my rational and logical way of engaging with Him. The first was when I felt Him say to me, "You think that seeing is believing, but

I tell you, believe and then you will see." This is something that I have found true about a number of aspects of my faith. Until I let go of my desire for understanding and rationality, certain things did not make sense. When I simply accepted those aspects as they were, I began to understand.

An example of where I struggled with this issue was around my understanding of something that was going on in me at a very real, but very spiritual level. It was a point in time where I started to speak in tongues. This was not something I went seeking. I had actually had a number of experiences earlier in life that had quite put me off the whole idea. I felt that it was not something for me.

I went through a period of time, however, where a desire kept welling up in me more and more persistently. It was a feeling that I just needed to let all this *babbling* come out of me. I felt really uncomfortable about it as it reminded me of being a child when we used to play games that we could speak in different languages by simply uttering random syllables. It just didn't make sense to me and seemed very weird. Why would God want me to speak stuff neither I nor anyone around me could understand? As I grappled with this and even shared my feelings with others, I felt God's gentle chastisement, "Do you have to understand everything about Me and what I do before you will accept it?"

As time went on and I began to use the gift, I did start to find that it made more sense, and that it had value in many aspects of my faith life. My understanding grew as I responded in cooperation with God. In fact, I now find praying in tongues invaluable in helping me to know how to pray about many situations, taking me to a different position, seeing more in the Spirit than in the natural realm. It also helps me to overcome my natural thinking and emotions in times of difficulty where I struggle to pray at all.

The same has been true of my understanding of our purpose and the meaning of our existence here. When I started to realise that the Bible wasn't a book of stories but pieces of the one story of the interaction of God with His creation; that it wasn't about me or us, but about God, I also started to understand many other aspects of my faith that had previously been unclear. However, again, that required my letting go of some previously held beliefs that were not congruent or compatible with the new understanding. It also required illumination that only the Holy Spirit can give.

Letting go of human ways of thinking and responding is not an easy task. We are constantly and consistently bombarded with attitudes and beliefs that are far more *natural* and effortless to follow in many ways. They also give a great appearance of promising abundant life and freedom to be and have all we want. I have come to realise more and more clearly, however, the lie that is presented to us, and the fact that most, if not all of these promises are very shallow, or only thin shells masking the road to bondage and death.

Standing at the crossroads, the road that leads to death appears very glossy, exciting and full of promise. It really looks as though it will bring you a great life. The road leading to life seems quiet, unassuming, humble and small, and promising very little rather than restriction and isolation. It is not until you travel a little further that you realise that choosing the road away from God leads to serving something that will never be satisfied and will never give satisfaction; this is actually the bondage.

Losing the world means that I can no longer care what friends or even family think of my decisions and actions. Over the past years, following God's prompting has meant that I have done less in terms of ministry and *working*. There have been many times where I have wondered whether I am hearing wrong, am simply lazy or in some other way dysfunctional. I do know that much of what I have been learning, however, is how to BE.

So much of our teaching both within and without church circles is that we must do, we must find what we are supposed to do, do it with all our energy and passion, and do it well. While I don't disagree with this in one sense, there is a major problem when this becomes about our acceptance, value and worth – what we offer to others, to the world. The last few years, God has brought me back again and again to a place where He questions my motives on what I desire to *do*, and asks me to rest in *being*. I am learning to work from a place of rest.

A revelation that has become more and more clear to me is that *who we are* impacts the Kingdom of Heaven far more than *what we do*. As I have heard prophetic words about a time to come where people are being drawn to Christians in the street, wanting what they have, I have realised that the more we radiate and exude Christ from our being as we are further filled with His Spirit and transformed into His likeness, the more attractive we become to those who are seeking. Counter to our *intuition* and logic, we won't need to go about doing, as such, but simply responding to those who come knocking. Again, it is not something we can do for ourselves, but I believe it will happen naturally as we draw closer to God and spend more time with Him.

If you would like to explore more about the differences between the *world's way* and God's way of how the world works, I have written, *Untruth: Exploring Truth in a Post Truth World,* a book which unpacks some of our most commonly held beliefs and understanding, holding them up to deeper scrutiny.

Questions for further reflection and action

1. What areas of your own thinking and behaving has God transformed already?

2. Can you identify thought patterns and beliefs you have that are still more attuned to the world's way of operating than God's truths? What verses from Scripture can you use to replace the lies with God's truth?

3. As someone who carries the Spirit of Christ, how will you endeavour to extend the Kingdom of God wherever you go? And if you are not sure whether you carry the Spirit of Christ, why not invite Holy Spirit to dwell in you now?

4. Spend some time meditating on the scriptures at the beginning of this chapter. What does God want to say to you through them?

Handing Back Control of Offence

"The mouth speaks what the heart is full of." Luke 6:45
"Whoever would foster love covers over an offense…" Proverbs 17:9
"A person's wisdom yields patience; it is to one's glory to overlook an offense."
Proverbs 19:11

"Get off the road, moron!"

"Where'dya get your licence, off the back of a cereal box?"

These were just a couple of examples of my repertoire when it came to driving. Although I hadn't developed full blown road rage – I kept my rants to the privacy of my car – I had little patience with the habits and mistakes of others on the road. Since the birth of my daughter, my language had changed a little. Let's face it, none of us want the ignominy of our children repeating certain words they have heard from their parents into other situations. Let me add, as an aside here, having a child also confronted me on language: if we don't think it sounds good coming out of the mouth of a two or three-year-old, what makes it any better coming from an adult?

Until I did a course where we discussed the idea of how we talk both with and about others, pointing out that there are really only two types of words we speak over and into others' lives – blessings or curses – I didn't really think about the amount of negativity my attitudes and behaviours generated. If I thought about it at all, it was either in terms of "They deserve it, they should do better", or "I'm just letting off steam/frustration."

I didn't really believe that my words had any power or effect, but thinking about it, even at a basic, scientific level, we know that we take on board so much of what others say to us. If we perceive negative things about ourselves, through advertising and other media, or other people's words and attitudes, we easily believe this is the truth. How much more does what we speak colour, reinforce and deepen our beliefs about, or attitudes to others? This doesn't even take into account the idea that words have creative power, either for building up or tearing down.

All this aside, I realised that much of my response to others came from an underlying sense of offense. As with many other aspects of my behaviour, I could see this as having a protective element to it, also. By taking offence to what you said or did, I could make it about you, not my own lack or failings. It protected me (or so I thought) from the hurt I may have felt by what you said or did.

Similar to unforgiveness, offence wants to see retribution, usually in the form of punishment of the other, or vindication of myself. It played a huge role in my life as a primary response to others, always ready to spring up in me at a moment's notice as soon as I got a sniff of anything I could remotely interpret as offensive. Like a mother sniffing out dirty socks in a teenager's room, I could spot offence at fifty paces or more. Unfortunately, I didn't realise that my vision was actually quite cloudy, and much that I interpreted as offensive was either not intended that way, or was even non-existent.

What I did realise in the middle of this was that I could be part of the solution, rather than simply adding to the problem. Take the example of driving again. I remember the challenge to bless people, to speak words of blessing over people when they offended me in some way, rather than speaking negative words, or cursing them.

As I started to practise this, I recognised, two things. One was that sometimes people (even me!) make mistakes while they are driving (or doing anything else, for that matter), and it is not necessarily a character trait or consistent behaviour. I could drive, and live, spreading grace toward people rather than negativity (even if they were unaware of it), and at least I would come out feeling a lot happier at the end of the day.

The second was a little tongue-in-cheek, but the point is similar. If a person is driving in a reckless and dangerous way, not caring about others around them, chances are they have enough issues and problems going on in their life without me adding to it. Rather than throwing abuse at them, I can throw blessings at them, and hopefully they have a better day. It may even change outcomes in their day.

Actioning both these concepts in my life have been part of a growing awareness of my role in this world as a *Christ-bearer*. Rather than being someone to judge and condemn the world, my desire is to carry God's Kingdom in me in all its fullness, so that it slops out wherever I go.

Another incident that took the issue to a whole new level for me was realising that offence wasn't just an physiological emotion or attitude, but that, as with many aspects of life, it can carry a spiritual aspect.

The situation that really highlighted this for me was coming home from a date night one evening. It had been a lovely evening — dinner followed by a movie and we had enjoyed relaxing in each other's company. On the way home, we stopped off for milk at a local supermarket. The suburb is at the end of the train line, and has a particular atmosphere and characteristics often associated with such places. A number of groups of people were hanging about drinking and smoking and my usual smile didn't get a similar response. I actually felt quite uncomfortable and quickly made my purchase and left.

As we drove the further ten minutes or so up the mountain to our home, we continued our conversation. However, as we talked, one of us misunderstood the other, which elicited a further negative response, and before we knew it, we were both feeling highly offended with each other. It wasn't until the next morning that I realised I hadn't just picked up milk at the supermarket, but that offence had jumped into the car with me. Having learnt some great methods of dealing with external spiritual garbage, we immediately agreed that we were not going to partner with offence and sent it to the foot of the cross and the problem was gone.

I'm not one for blaming the enemy for every negative emotion, but there are times when it has become obvious to me that emotional states are external rather than internal. If I have dealt with my part in the situation, making sure I have forgiven who I need to, or apologised if I am at fault, and the emotion still won't move, chances are it is not mine to deal with and stating I won't partner with it usually shifts it immediately.

Questions for further reflection and action

1. Can you think of times you have decided to forgive someone, or let go of offence? What was the outcome?

2. Are there circumstances in your life where you need to let go of offence or forgive someone? Read Matt 18:21-35 if you are struggling, and reflect on what sort of torture unforgiveness may add to your life. Speak out your forgiveness as an act of your will.

3. Are you aware of *partnering with* offence, or using it as a protection mechanism? If you are, breaking your agreement with offence can quickly change your outlook on life!

4. Spend some time meditating on the scriptures at the beginning of this chapter. What does God want to say to you through them?

Handing Back Control of Structure

""For my thoughts are not your thoughts, neither are your ways my ways," declares the Lord." Isaiah 55:8
"Come to me, all you who are weary and burdened, and I will give you rest. Take my yoke upon you and learn from me, for I am gentle and humble in heart, and you will find rest for your souls. For my yoke is easy and my burden is light." Matt 11:28-30

Structure and process have become a seemingly efficient and necessary method to deal with larger enterprises and organisations. Even as I was growing up, my mother's way of dealing with five kids was to have a number of practises to sort out the various requirements of running the home. This included having specific days she did certain things, from washing towels and each person's bedding, to meal times and bedtimes, which at times could be quite rigid. I do remember her saying to me when I became a parent, that if you had routine, even if everything went haywire, or you were out late, when you got home and were able to, you could slip back into that routine, for example, of dinner, bath and bed, and it would have a calming effect on children.

There is much truth in this. Routine can make us feel safe and secure, and *under control*. However, it can also become inhibiting and instead of helping us, take over our lives. Indeed, the unhelpful end of the spectrum of routines begins to look like obsessive compulsive disorder, where the individual has to go through set routines that may have little or no actual purpose other than to make the person feel safe.

Personally, my husband felt I was a little over structured and controlling when it came to some of my routines and processes when we married. However, when I completed the Hermann Brain Dominance Instrument as part of his training in the same, what was going on for me became clearer. It revealed that a high level of process was something I slipped into when I was feeling stressed. Crossing every "t" and dotting every "i", or otherwise making sure that everything was *as it should be*, helped me to feel in control and safe. The problem was not so much with having processes and structures as this issue of them becoming rigid and inflexible to the point where they became the driver. When the process becomes more important than the outcome we are trying to achieve, it can cause more problems than it solves.

A few years back, I went through a period where God kept on my case about this, digging me deeper into exploring and understanding a new way of living. While it had started earlier, as I was only just beginning to even be able to put any words to what I was sensing, we had a *chance encounter* with someone in Uganda.

The host of the guest house where we spent our first night placed her at our breakfast table the very first morning we were in the country. As we talked, we found we had much in common, from the superficial to deeper aspects of our faith, even to the ministry she was doing among refugees. As we shared with each other, she began speaking prophetically over my life. Funnily enough, (God's sense of humour, I think), it was about letting go of control of various aspects of my life, but structure and process were central in it all, as well as my *need to know*, which I was just beginning to untangle.

A couple of months later, I was at the chiropractor, and he was talking about the interesting ways in which different people's bodies responded to damage and weaknesses. He observed that my *stabilizing* muscles around my hips and lower back were requiring a great deal of hard work to loosen them at all. Further, he said that when I had any inflammation or damage in my lower back, these stabilizing muscles would immediately go into overdrive, even if my back wasn't that bad. I wrote in my journal at the time, *"I felt this was a physical representation of how I respond emotionally and spiritually. Any emotional or spiritual pain or disruption has me uptight and overly concerned. This is not a place of rest, but comes back again to control. I get a picture like when you are driving a car. If bad road conditions caused an accident, you become overly cautious about every bump, every gravel patch and pothole, making sure you steer extra carefully, gripping the steering wheel too tightly, in the end turning what was a little bump into something that almost stalls you, leading to fear and a lack of forward motion."*

Shortly after this, I was talking with a friend about the journey I was on. We were both involved with the same prayer ministry team. As we had been training, I had needed to deal with myself about her methodology as compared to mine. I was very structured and followed the steps as per our training, whereas I felt she was all over the place. However, I had come to a place where I could let that go, I could allow her to be herself and even celebrate it. I was actually coming to a place of working out how letting go like that *worked* for me, what it might look like.

Still thinking about all this as I left and drove home, God gave me another picture. It tied in with a comment someone had made decades before about the way they used their playpen. Rather than putting the kids in it, they had used it when they were doing the ironing, to protect the kids from pulling the iron on their heads, or otherwise burning themselves. In my picture, I was in the playpen, at first as a small child, and then as that adult, doing the ironing. What I felt God showing me was that although we can use structures (like a playpen) to keep people safe, there is also a point at which it starts to inhibit you from freely operating as you should. For me, this was specifically around the prayer ministry at that time, but God has since been expanding this into many other areas.

My discussion with God (and my friend) had been along the lines of the idea that as Christian organisations and ministries, we put structures in place to protect both the workers and the client/member. However, if these are too rigid, too prescriptive, we end can up inhibiting Holy Spirit. As we move into what many are calling a new era, I believe this is something essential for us to grasp. For me it has been a journey of trust. Learning to trust others is one aspect, but far greater, it is growing my trust in God.

When everything looks out of control in the natural sense, do I still trust God?

It comes back to our understanding, beliefs and theology around Holy Spirit. I have been involved with a number of church communities and ministries over the past couple of decades where many use the descriptor *Spirit-led* quite freely. However, there seem to be two extremes (as usual) of what this might mean. On one side, it generally seems to only go so far as it fits with the leadership's idea of what Holy Spirit may or may not being doing or saying. On the other, anything and everything goes, sometimes without any discernment seeming to be in use. Perhaps this is what some leadership fears, which has led to the creation of so many structures.

A question I have further been pondering on is how we view each other in terms of the concept of Holy Spirit dwelling in each of us. I believe we tend to make our own judgements about whether others have the Holy Spirit, particularly those who we don't know well. Just check out some of the conversations on social media! What I think we are doing though, is trying to control others, or situations where we don't feel safe rather than trusting God with what He is doing. There needs to be some balance of using discernment, and how we enact that is just as important. Do we shut people down, or do we walk a little closer with them? What situations do we create to offer people a place to test their gifts *within the playpen* until they have matured? This leads to another aspect where we (the Church) seem to have grave difficulty making distinctions – there is a vast difference between maturity in character and giftedness. For far too long, we have elevated the gifted without dealing with character issues. The devastating results of this show up regularly in the number of prominent leaders who end up in relational, financial or addiction messes, a combination of the three, or simply walk away from faith altogether.

I think that what is probably most important here is further teaching on actually listening to and asking Holy Spirit ourselves before accepting everything that said to us by another with the tag line of "this is what God is saying" as truly what God is saying. We need to test what people say to us, both through the light of Scripture and through our own relationship with God. This includes asking whether the word is relevant to me and my situation particularly, especially when I desperately want it to be. I know I have been on the receiving end of a *word from God* that took me off on a little rabbit trail. The problem was, it tapped into some of the desires of my heart that God had already shown me He was not going to fulfill the way I thought. As soon as I went back to God about it, I realised the word was a distraction and very little, if any, was from God.

In my last round of formal studies, the course I took investigated church practices in the light of the Bible, traditions and various theologies. Within the course, we each had a level of freedom to explore aspects we had particular interest in. For me, much of this came back to the structure of church that many see as vital and unchangeable. Where we can get tripped up, though, is that much of what we interpret through Scripture comes with a heavy dose of cultural and historical bias. The story of Jesus illustrates the issue clearly. The scholars and priests of the day had investigated Scripture to the depths, particularly the prophetic words. They knew the promise of salvation, of a Saviour inside out. And many had a clear picture of what they hoped this would look like: a strong leader coming with an army to free them from the tyranny of Rome. Jesus, however, came quietly, as a baby, and as a servant. His Kingdom was and is upside down in many ways to how the world operates. Many of the issues the Jewish people hoped Messiah would come and deal with, He did not, or at least, He didn't deal with them the way they wanted Him to. The freedom they were hoping would always have limitations, whereas the freedom He brought was *unlimitable*.

In their essence, most structures we have wrapped around our idea of *church*, even those which we might like to believe are about keeping people *safe*, actually stifle and suppress much that Holy Spirit would like to do. Our processes to keep the faith *pure*, to be *excellent* in what we do are far more about what people think than what God wants for us. So often I have heard pastors and leaders talk about wanting to lengthen worship or prayer time, or even the service time but they won't because people in the congregation will get upset, leave or stop coming. My experience in life as well as my observations of Scripture is that when Jesus turns up, many get offended, uncomfortable and want to leave.

Over the past few years, many people have been hearing God say that He is doing a new thing, quoting Isaiah 43:19. More recently, as we have wondered what this might look like, numbers of us have come to the same conclusion. If it is something new, something we have never seen before, then until it comes, we are unlikely to get much of an inkling of what it is. We need to wait, trusting that when the new comes, Holy Spirit is able to make sure we see it. We also need to be light on our feet, ready to move and not inhibited by the structures of the past.

In addition to all this, I have also been on a journey through the last couple of years with God speaking to me about worldly structures. Through the removal of a enormous tree out the front of our home, which was full of termites, I saw a parallel with earthly governance structures that are becoming very unstable, not the least because they are eating themselves away from the inside. The pervasiveness of corruption is causing instability that threatens not only to bring the whole structure down, but also has the possibility of causing a great deal of destruction on its way. What I felt God showing me through this example is that He has the power to not only bring them down safely (as the tree removalists brought the trees outside our property down safely a week before a massive storm!), but that He could also bring provision for His people through it all – we now have about ten years supply of wood for our fire. As I questioned Him about what might happen with a lack of structure in our society, seeing only anarchy as the answer, He told me that even now He is raising up other structures to replace the corrupt ones, with people who will truly serve God and society rather than themselves. I am still not sure exactly how all this will happen. However, one operational strategy He is giving me are the words *unconditional generosity*, which is giving to others with no thought for what they may or may not provide for me (material or otherwise) in return. The idea is to trust in His provision to the point where I don't need to hold anything back from others. It is in stark opposition to the way the world currently operates, which is to hold as much back to self as possible, always expecting others to *pay back what they owe us*. Years ago, I read a book that suggested the mark of the beast had to do with greed. To me, this suggests a powerful opposite to greed. Hold everything lightly. It also fits in very well with Jesus' words about giving your coat as well as your shirt and walking two miles when someone asks you to go one.

Jesus was a radical and His Kingdom is one of radically different behaviour and attitudes. When I first started this book, I was going to call it *Losing my life and loving it* until I found someone else had already used that title. However, it does tie in well with Jesus' words about losing our life if we hold onto it but gaining the world if we let go of all we hold dear, (Mark 8:34-37). Yes, sometimes He does give it back to us, but we need to let go without that thought in mind. We need to let go and cut the strings, cut the ties, cut our ability to be able to grab it back again. It is in this place that we find true freedom.

Questions for further reflection and action

1. What structures are you aware of in your life that you use to make you feel safe?

2. Ask Holy Spirit to reveal to you any structures that it is time for you to let go of.

3. How might your life change if you had spaces where there was more freedom and less structure? Would you be willing to set aside time to explore life less structured?

4. Spend some time meditating on the scriptures at the beginning of this chapter. What does God want to say to you through them?

Handing Back Control of My Reputation

"Blessed are you when people insult you, persecute you and falsely say all kinds of evil against you because of me." Matt 5:11

"If anyone would come after me he must deny himself and take up his cross and follow me. For whoever wants to save his life will lose it, but whoever loses his life for me and for the Gospel will save it." Mark 8:34, 35

"...he made himself nothing by taking the very nature of a servant, being made in human likeness." Phil 2:7

"Humble yourselves, therefore, under God's mighty hand, that he may lift you up in due time." 1 Peter 5:6

I have a vivid recollection of a phone call one Saturday morning in my early twenties. The caller identified himself as being from the local police and he wanted to talk with me about a friend who had allegedly been involved in some untoward behaviour the night before. Even as I racked my brain to think of what he might have done that would warrant police involvement, I immediately went to his defence: "No, he would never do something like that; it's not the sort of person he is". I was in shock that anyone could accuse my friend of such things, that someone could attack his reputation in such a way. Eventually the caller began to wrap up the call, saying, "Just one last question for you, what's today's date?" It was April 1st and in my Saturday morning stupor, I had not even recognised the voice of another friend acting as the supposed policeman.

A reputation is one of the easiest things to destroy, and one of the hardest to repair. The attack on reputations seems to be a favourite political ploy in this season. Just cast enough doubt, say something loud enough and long enough at it must be at least a little bit true, surely? Even if the mud doesn't quite stick, it tends to leave a stain, a mark, a doubt: What if it is true? And our belief in the adage, "Where there is smoke, there is fire" adds to the doubt. Is it any wonder, in the age of social media, we have children as young as twelve who are concerned about creating an online *brand*, and their greatest fear is damage to their *brand*. It is all wrapped up in reputation and identity, clothed loosely in image. What is the image I project into the world, and is that the same as my identity? And if someone decides to destroy my reputation, what does that do to my identity?

One of the earliest attacks on my identity and reputation occurred when I was about nine years old. I remember those I had considered friends turning on me and joining in with some quite nasty name calling. I felt betrayed, rejected and confused. Even more, a place I had felt safe in was suddenly no longer safe. Added to this was a layer of shame, a sense that there was something inherently wrong with me. It was the beginning of a distinct change for me in my relationships with others. I started to learn that not everyone was trustworthy and was probably an early brick in the protective wall I started to build around my heart.

Over the years, there have been many further incidences where my sense of my identity and hence my reputation felt under attack. For anyone who has experienced this (which is probably all of us at some point in time), it is a bewildering and painful experience. Our immediate instinct is to fight back. We want to say, "*you are!*", or use other language or even our bodies to get off the back foot and onto the offense. Inherently, we yearn to prove that we are ok, that we are better than the way we are being portrayed, if not better than the accuser.

Through my teens, like many, I struggled with what sort of reputation I wanted, or didn't, as various others tried to pin labels and images to me. Some were about my outward appearance, my family and eventually my personality. While I pushed back to try to prove I was not who they said, underneath I was not only trying to have a *good reputation*, (whatever that might mean), but also work out who I really was. In many ways, I tried to distance myself from my family as I had learnt early on that there were aspects of my family that I didn't feel helped my social status at least in the mêlée of teen angst. I measured my reputation almost entirely through what I sensed reflected back at me in the eyes of my peers. It was very shaky ground.

As I traversed into early adulthood and my relational circles changed, I felt more accepted, however every encounter with others still impacted how I felt about myself. It was an emotional rollercoaster. At some subconscious level, I believed getting married would give me the endorsement I was looking for. It would show everyone I was ok, and the love of a husband would be enough to keep me feeling good. But that external measuring stick was not going away in a hurry.

Looking back over this period, I realise that as much as I wanted a *good reputation* among people, my methodology was quite fickle. And, of course, when my marriage ended, it all came crashing down. So many of my beliefs about myself and my standing in the world were wrapped up in this image and my perceptions from others. I realised just how shaky those foundations were.

Heading to the welfare office after my marriage ended was another confrontation of my perceptions around reputation. I was shocked at my inner response of humiliation at how I appeared. I wasn't *one of those women*. My assessment of what it meant to be a single mum illuminated my pride in technicolour! In stark contrast, shame and pride walked together. I was ashamed of *how I looked*, or where I had landed, but my pride kept telling me that my image and reputation was all up to me, that I actually had the power to make it what I wanted.

Blaming others for where I landed, making it their issue not mine, helped shore up my damaged pride somewhat. In one sense, it was a period of time where I found a measure of healing in realising that other people's behaviour did not have to impact my identity, that I didn't have to wear other people's stuff. It helped at one level, but at another level, it was simply a different set of clothes to cover my fear of the nakedness of shame around what I believed was my true identity.

Much of this issue was relegated to the back burner, though, as God dealt with a number of other problems with my life foundations, as discussed elsewhere in this book. However, nothing in these matters is really separate. As mentioned earlier, our reputation with people can be so quickly and easily destroyed no matter how well things appear to be on the surface. How do we deal with this?

In past eras, our identity was very much wrapped up in our family. Protecting the family name was important in how we interacted with the rest of society – our acceptability, and hence our reputation. Looking at the Bible, though, it is obvious this is not a new problem. If prophets and kings of the Old Testament, disciples and even Jesus, had their reputations tarnished or destroyed, why would it be any different for us?

Recently, God has put His finger on this melding of reputation and identity in me again. As we have been through a disintegration of relationship within our church community, with no openings for restoration or even discussion, as well as a number of other relational issues, I became aware of God shining His spotlight on my behaviour. Although it was a lot less overt than the past, He showed me that some of my conversations were subtle requests to others to let me know that I was ok, that I was still acceptable, or even *in the right*. I hadn't been looking directly for validation, but skirting around the edges, looking to people instead of God. In the middle of some quite overt attacks on our reputation, which almost destroyed some relationships we thought were quite solid, I was learning I can't control my reputation in the eyes of others. But what does it look like to hand my reputation into God's control?

A central part of my growth in this area some years back included understanding the concept of integrity more deeply. Realising that this is about my responses and behaviours in every single scenario of my life, even those that no one else knows about has given me a good way to handle it. What I will do if I don't think anyone will find out is a true measure of who I am. Both my identity and my integrity ride on this. It shows up who I truly am when I don't think I am performing for someone. Obviously God always knows, but sometimes we like to pretend He doesn't really notice or care.

I still remember an *aha* moment of seeing the link between integrity and wholeness — a lack of integrity means we are not whole. But we also use that term about structures. If they have a lack of integrity, they are liable to collapse. It's the same with our identity. Without integrity, it is liable to collapse. This is further related to the Hebrew concept of *shalom*. While this is usually interpreted *peace* in the Bible it carries so much more richness than this. Shalom is also related to wholeness — nothing is missing. Further, it includes the idea of healing, restoration and restitution. There is a sense of return to created or Kingdom order — true peace.

The conclusion I come to about my reputation is that it is actually the wrong focus. There are times when doing what is right in God's eyes is going to cause issues with how others see me. To survive this, I need to be so grounded, my foundations need to be so firm that nothing can shake me from the conviction of who I am — my identity — in Jesus. After all, reputation is related to the opinion of others. Do I place their opinion on the highest pedestal? Scarily, that would raise them above God.

Alongside these issues, as we have negotiated the last couple of years, and particularly the last few months, I have come to a stark realisation that there is actually quite a famine in the realm of justice and righteousness at this time. Perhaps it is a clear sign of the times. As I have sought God around some of our personal situations and the lack of justice when confronting illegal and unethical behaviour in government agencies, as well as knowing others who are struggling with similar in the courts, even hearing it from lawyers, He took me back to the Old Testament prophets. Is 59:14-15 is quite explicit: *"So justice is driven back, and righteousness stands at a distance; truth has stumbled in the streets, honesty cannot enter. Truth is nowhere to be found, and whoever shuns evil becomes a prey."*

While this hasn't fixed my problem, it has given me rest. I cannot change this injustice. Indeed, in a court situation with a friend where injustice seemed to win the day again, there is a point at which we will just exhaust ourselves if we continue to try to fight this injustice simply using human means. I believe it has deep spiritual ties, and as such needs spiritual methods to deal with it. In the end, I do believe that we need to hold on to Romans 12:19 (CJB), "*Adonai* [the Lord] *says, 'Vengeance is my responsibility; I will repay."* We are incapable of judging rightly in many ways. Our personal hurt alongside our inability to know every aspect of the situation leave us biased at least.

In this season it is all the more important to keep our eyes on our Heavenly Father and what He is doing, rather than the thrashing about of the enemy. I do sense that this heightened and even more obvious activity is more like death throes than something we are to fear. Keeping ourselves closely hidden in God is our antidote.

Even as I was writing this chapter, a friend unknowingly gave me a picture that shows the issue very clearly. She saw an old-fashioned set of scales and I was standing on one of the plates. On the other side, God was putting the weights to show His measure of me. At the same time, others were throwing something like tennis balls to me, and I was either trying to put them on my side or God's. Her comment was that I actually needed to hit these balls away as they were a distraction. However, I also saw that when I try to add in other people's *weigh in* to God's weights, everything gets out of balance. If I want to stay on an even keel, the only measure I need is His.

Coming back to the problem of my identity and reputation, I am reminded of a period of time earlier when I was going through much healing. I commented to God that I felt like He was digging up all my foundations. I sensed Him grinning and His response was, "*Not quite all, just the ones that need it*". Having had a house with underpinning issues, where the foundations had shifted, it can be rather disarming when it feels as though the whole house is shifting under your feet. However, the end product is one that is far more stable. The picture I had in this scenario was of my feet on an increasingly large, stable Rock. Not because Jesus changes, but because, as I get to know Him better, my footing becomes firmer and I have more confidence in who He is. This is the only safe place in a time when all else seems to be shifting sand.

Questions for further reflection and action

1. Can you think of times your reputation has been in question? How did you feel? What did you do?

2. How does your reputation link to you identity today? Is it time to break some of those connectors? If so, ask Holy Spirit to reveal to you how you should do that and what He wants to do in that space.

3. Does your identity need to experience more of God's shalom? Ask Him what He would like to give you today.

4. Spend some time meditating on the scriptures at the beginning of this chapter. What does God want to say to you through them?

Life Restored

"I will restore to you the years that the swarming locust has eaten…" Joel 2:25

This promise in Joel has not only been a promise that I have held on to, but it has proven out in my life. As much as letting go has often felt like losing everything, the ways in which so much more has been returned or restored are just as countless. I may have felt I was giving up something very valuable to me, but I have learnt that God's graciousness and mercy means that He gives me so much more in return, with far greater value. He is also adjusting my lens to see value through His eyes, instead of my own.

So far, this book has been about letting go of those things that are not mine to control. In a nutshell, it is really about submission to God, allowing Him to have His place as Lord over every aspect of my life. Along my journey, in amongst the healing, has been a growing awareness of the spiritual battle we are in and the lies we have believed, even as Christians. While our journey with God is about learning to submit in increasing measure to Him, it is also about increasing in our authority under God. In releasing those aspects of our desires and behaviours where we try to take authority over God or what is only His to authorise, we do not abdicate all authority. There is authority we have been given that is ours to exercise.

One of the most helpful theology books I have read is *"I Give You Authority"*, by Charles Kraft. Kraft explains the authority God created us to have and what went wrong:

> *"At creation, therefore, authority of several kinds was given to Adam and Eve: authority to carry the image of God; authority to create children in God's image; authority over all creation. All would have gone well – with God over everything, humans under Him and angels serving them both – if God's enemy, Lucifer, had not succeeded in enticing Adam to misuse his authority by giving it all away."*[3]

Authority is a word that many people misinterpret to mean *aggressive dominance for self-aggrandisement*. We tend to look at people who have misused authority rather than seeing authority as a responsibility. I think this is the reason many people struggle with God. They view Him as a megalomaniac, trying to subdue and dominate people, to bend them to His will for His purposes. In the same way, they can interpret Genesis 1:26 about making *man* in God's image, and even the verses about women submitting to men through the same misunderstanding, ending up with a very skewed view of what was created to be glorious. The point I keep coming back to myself is that God created good. It is the accuser who has tried to destroy everything that was good. In Christ, we can reclaim the way things God originally intended them to be.

For me, this means recognising that I don't have to live under the lies of the enemy. Using my authority as someone whom the Spirit of Jesus lives in, I can reclaim joy, peace, wholeness, purpose, and all the fruit of the Spirit. When I am assured of who I am in Christ, of all He has done for me, I can live in submission to other people and to God, knowing that it doesn't diminish me one iota. I am who

---

3. Extract from *I Give You Authority: Practicing The Authority Jesus Gave Us*, © Charles H. Kraft 1997, Chosen Books, p 20

I am because God created me that way for a purpose and I know what that is. However, I can also stand up in authority instead of submission to the enemy. As the father of lies, nothing he tells me is truth, so when I start hearing or thinking things that don't add up with the Word of God, I can reject them with authority. When things happen in my life and around me that don't add up with the Word of God, I can declare the Word of God into those areas. I don't have to accept everything thrown my way by the brokenness of the world or other people, or from the spirit world.

To some people, this might sound a little wacky. To me, when I first started practising it, it seemed a little wacky too. However, it has been life changing. At the very least, a big change for me has been taking authority over what I choose to believe. Some of those things have been so ingrained, so much a part of my entire life (even generational), that it has been very difficult to choose to believe something different. I am sure there are still areas that are changing and that need to change.

As an example, one of those beliefs has been about my 'smallness.' Although this has probably been partially affected by my stature (being a gigantic 154cm… yes, I do scrape over the five foot mark!), the underlying message I lived with for many years was that I was no one important, no one special, that I didn't deserve anything, that I was easy to overlook. How disempowering! It took me a long time to be able to accept the Word of God at face value, words such as Psalm 139. Although I believed the Bible in a general sense and could tell others to believe these sorts of words about themselves with great conviction, deep down I struggled take it on board for myself.

Over a period of time where I went through deep healing; healing that went beyond my emotional state, where I dealt with spiritual issues such as vows and curses and even broken promises, I started to claim back, in the authority of Jesus' name, that which was mine, that which the enemy of my soul had stolen. At first, I couldn't do it by myself or even for myself. There were times where I complied with the instructions, but didn't really believe that words had that much power. How wrong I was. I have had so many instances where I couldn't tell you exactly what happened or what changed, but where, over a period of time, I have realised that I am free; I am not operating the same way anymore. A perfect example of this was to do with anxiety.

I had never considered myself a particularly anxious person. However, looking back, I realise my anxiety was obvious to others much of the time. This impacted me numerous ways from emotional to physical, including headaches that were generally only alleviated by sleep, and it was also probably a significant factor in the clinical depression I endured for four years.

At the time, I wasn't particularly seeking healing from anxiety, or even aware that this was not a normal way to live. However, one morning I woke up with a considerable sense of anxiety with the accompanying threatening headache. It struck me particularly because I couldn't think of anything that would cause me anxiety at that point, so in my semi-awake phase, I asked God to show me what was causing this anxiety. The story of my birth came into my mind.

My parents lived on a dairy farm when I was born, with some distance to travel into town to the hospital. On the way, at about 3 am, the car broke down. Now, I had always heard the story from my father's perspective. He left my mother in the car and walked to the nearest farm. A woman was there alone (her husband was away) and was none too happy about getting up to a man at her front door at that time of the night. However, eventually she allowed my father to take the only available vehicle, a truck, which was somewhere else and he had to go and get it. On finding the truck, he returned to get my mother, taking her to the hospital, where I was born about half an hour later.

As I was reflecting on this, I heard the question, "What was happening for your mother at that time?" I suddenly saw the situation from her perspective. How must she have felt, sitting in the dark completely alone? There were no mobile phones then, and even many homes did not have a phone. She had already had two children as well as a nursing background, so must have known that my arrival was imminent. I would guess her major emotion at that time would have been a considerable dose of… anxiety! Was she going to have this baby here on her own in the dark? What had happened to her husband? What should she do? What would she do if…?

At that moment, I realised how this must have impacted me as an unborn baby; I believe that God was showing me that this was the time at which anxiety became a base or underlying issue for me.

The anxiety continued to hover around me that morning as I headed to a Bible College class. At the beginning of our class, we spent time in groups praying for each other. I shared the story with my group and they prayed for me and I didn't think much of it. It was only a couple of months later that I realised that something had changed.

Martin and I had been dating for a couple of years. We had come to a point where we had decided to make the big commitment of marriage. That was in October. We decided that the beginning of the school year would be the best time for all the changes that would occur for my daughter, which meant an early January wedding. We had about three months.

In that time, we needed to finish some work on my house to prepare it for sale, sell it, prepare for a wedding (including our marriage prep classes), clean out the excesses of two houses to combine them into one, finish a course we were doing (which was pretty intense) and I was doing a couple of classes at Bible College with work to finish for the end of semester. It was in the midst of this that I realised I had been healed. Usually, half this amount of stress would have had me in a tizz, probably with several bouts of those headaches. However, I had nothing but peace. I couldn't have been more laid back about it all. It was around this time that I also came to a place of believing that I would not suffer depression in the same way again. A couple of decades on, that has proven out.

The point is, there are many things in life that we simply put up with because someone has told us we that we shouldn't expect more. It might be that we grow up believing that we shouldn't expect too much out of life, or that everyone has to go through these things, however, the reality is, many of them are simply lies, especially when they relate to false beliefs.

I am not saying that Christians shouldn't have problems, difficulty or suffering. Far from it. It is not my personal experience and I don't believe it is Biblical — there are so many verses that talk about when we suffer, and have struggles not if. After all, without suffering, how would we develop perseverance, character and hope? (Romans 5:3,4) It is in the hard times that our faith has a chance to grow and develop. It is not the lack of difficulties that marks the Christian life, but the way we deal with them. To me,

Romans 8:18-39 sums it up perfectly:

> *"I consider that our present sufferings are not worth comparing with the glory that will be revealed in us. The creation waits in eager expectation for the sons of God to be revealed. For the creation was subjected to frustration, not by its own choice, but by the will of the one who subjected it, in hope that the creation itself will be liberated from its bondage to decay and brought into the glorious freedom of the children of God.*
>
> *We know that the whole creation has been groaning as in the pains of childbirth right up to the present time. Not only so, but we ourselves, who have the firstfruits of the Spirit, groan inwardly as we wait eagerly for our adoption as sons, the redemption of our bodies. For in this hope we were saved. But hope that is seen is no hope at all. Who hopes for what he already has? But if we hope for what we do not yet have, we wait for it patiently.*
>
> *In the same way, the Spirit helps us in our weakness. We do not know what we ought to pray for, but the Spirit himself intercedes for us with groans that words cannot express. And he who searches our hearts knows the mind of the Spirit, because the Spirit intercedes for the saints in accordance with God's will.*
>
> *And we know that in all things God works for the good of those who love him, who have been called according to his purpose. For those God foreknew he also predestined to be conformed to the likeness of his Son, that he might be the firstborn among many brothers. And those he predestined, he also called; those*

he called, he also justified; those he justified, he also glorified.

What, then, shall we say in response to this? If God is for us, who can be against us? He who did not spare his own Son, but gave him up for us all—how will he not also, along with him, graciously give us all things? Who will bring any charge against those whom God has chosen? It is God who justifies. Who is he that condemns? Christ Jesus, who died—more than that, who was raised to life—is at the right hand of God and is also interceding for us. Who shall separate us from the love of Christ? Shall trouble or hardship or persecution or famine or nakedness or danger or sword? As it is written: "For your sake we face death all day long; we are considered as sheep to be slaughtered." No, in all these things we are more than conquerors through him who loved us. For I am convinced that neither death nor life, neither angels nor demons, neither the present nor the future, nor any powers, neither height nor depth, nor anything else in all creation, will be able to separate us from the love of God that is in Christ Jesus our Lord."

Hallelujah!

Questions for further reflection and action:

1. What are the specific experiences you have had where God has restored something to you?

2. What would you like God to further restore in your life? Ask Him what He would like to do about anything that comes up.

3. What do you think your life would look like if you allowed Him to have complete control over every aspect of it?

Conclusion

Life is a journey of discovery. On it we may learn some things that are helpful and others that are not so helpful. As children, we are particularly vulnerable, as we do not have the same resources or maturity to discern between what is good and what is not. The outcome of what we learn is very much dependent on those who care for us in varieties of ways.

As we enter into and progress on our journey with God, we have access to perfect truth and goodness. The Holy Spirit shows us His ways, if we are open to hear. We may need to adjust some of our beliefs and attitudes, and may need varying amounts of healing to be able to take on new attitudes and behaviours. However, part of the journey includes our restoration to wholeness so that we have an account to give, a testimony of who Jesus is and what He has done for us. This also gives us compassion and opportunity to pass these blessings on to others who are struggling with similar issues.

In all honesty, Christianity should be easy to increase exponentially. If we were really convinced and sure about what God has done in our lives and if we have allowed Him to do the work of transforming us, then we should have no problem in sharing it with others. As we get to know Him at a deeper and deeper level, and become more and more whole, it should be easier and more compelling to want that for others, as well. Too often,

I think we are not confident in God, in who He is and what He wants to do for us and every individual on earth, and so we hold back. My challenge and desire is to offer hope and assurance to others that what God has done and continues to do in my life, He longs to do for you.

A major understanding I have come to, however, is that while we often come to God looking for Him to change that which is external to us, He is far more interested in bringing our internal life into His order. The more we live out of His order, the less ability the external has to impact us in negative ways. As we come into His order and His perspective, we both live in the Kingdom of God as well as live out of it. The realities of the Kingdom become more real to us than the realities of the world.

You will also have noticed that this book is also not a 'how to' book. I don't believe that there is a 'one size fits all' for healing and wholeness. God wants us each to partner with Him in our own relationship, rather than shadow someone else's journey. Our healing course is as individual as we are. Jesus promised us that He would send the Holy Spirit to teach us all things and be our guide. Our role is simply to stop, listen and follow this guidance. As much as this is not always easy, it is simple. My prayer for you, therefore, is that God would speak into your life in ways you can hear, and that He would surround you with others who clearly speak His words to you as well. May you continue to walk deeper and deeper into His ways until you are no longer aware of the wind and waves, but only His beautiful Presence.

If this book has stirred up areas for you that you know need healing and you are not sure where to head for help or support, please head to www.ruthembery.com for more information.

Postscript

I include the following as an example of God's grace, goodness and faithfulness in ways that are far more than we often dream of, and to affirm that nothing is beyond His ability. He is able to do far more than we can imagine.

As I have mentioned earlier, my relationship with my father was not easy or comfortable, especially in the last years of his life. There was a point at which I felt he had essentially disassociated from us as his family and although I kept some contact with him, I struggled to connect in any meaningful way.

In the middle of his seventieth year, he had a couple of incidents of hospitalisation. Having had juvenile diabetes from his mid-teens, simple illnesses could quickly become complicated. It was in one such incident that my older brother rang me to let me know my dad was in hospital and that this time it didn't look like he would come out. In fact, he was in a coma and medical staff felt it was days at the most. My brother was suggesting that if I wanted to see my dad before he died, it needed to be now.

My immediate response was that I didn't feel I needed to go.

The hospital was over two hours' drive away and I wasn't sure what purpose it would serve to go and see him. My brother suggested that I wouldn't want to have any regrets in this regard, but I really couldn't imagine what those regrets might look like.

After hanging up the phone, I went on my morning walk, and as I did, talked to God about what I should do. I thought about why I didn't feel any necessity to see my dad one last time, and as I did, I realised that in many ways, I had already given up on the relationship. I no longer saw any purpose or meaning in the relationship with my dad.

As I reflected on this, I suddenly found myself overwhelmed with grief. Trying to make sense of this unexpected response, I realised that my anguish, rather than being for what I was losing, was actually for what had not been, what I felt I had missed out on.

Understanding this, and moving through it, I did go to visit my dad before he died, as much as anything, probably out of respect for the fact that he still was my dad. As the family gathered around, several of us felt that God was saying that this would not end in death. Wanting to be sure that my dad had made his peace with God, given that I felt he had pretty much rejected the faith his parents had brought him up with, and held on deeply to for much of his earlier life, this was something I clung to. I had a little fantasy where he would open his eyes one last time and tell someone that he had made peace with God, and then he would die.

But it never happened.

Even though I felt so let down in many ways, I decided that I would like to give something of a eulogy at the funeral. I wanted to focus on the positives of who he was and what he did for us as his family, as I knew that there would be pitifully little else that would honour him. He had pretty much withdrawn from the world and it was a very small gathering to bid him farewell.

I found that, although I struggled to feel particularly thankful for these things, I could list a great many ways in which our dad had been a good dad, many of which I had taken pretty much for granted. Things such as always working hard to provide for us financially and materially; that he took us for family outings and holidays; that he brought us up to value education and faith, and to think for ourselves. Indeed, I nearly undid myself when I started by saying I had polished my shoes in honour of my dad – he was such a stickler for clean shoes.

The day of the funeral was difficult and uncomfortable on many fronts and I was glad when it was over and I could get back to *normal* life. However, God had not finished with me in this regard. Reading back through my journal from that time more recently, it took a few months more before I admitted, even to myself, the level of pain I had experienced, and how rejected I had felt by him.

There were two incidences that happened, though, that began to change all that.

One was an extremely awkward phone call from my dad's lady friend sometime later. I really didn't want to speak with her. I am sure she was feeling just as discomforted, telling me that she kept having this prompting to call me, and that she had no idea why, except to tell me that my dad had loved me very much; of how much he had spoken of me, with so much pride and love.

At that point, I knew exactly where her prompting was coming from and why she was ringing. I explained this to her through the tears I was now crying. Even though, at that point, there was still a part of me that wanted to deny it, the truth was starting to break through.

The second incident came about at the end of a day out four-wheel driving. Martin and I were almost home, when the most unusual feeling came over me. I had this sudden desire of "I wish I could have shared this day with my dad."

Those thoughts were not thoughts I had had in any of my adult life and they quite surprised me. What came next, though, was even stranger, as I suddenly got a very strong image of my father healthy, strong, fit and filled with joy enjoying the company of others. It was not a memory from earlier days, as he was not a young man in this picture. The sense I have, (and still believe), is that God gave me a glimpse of my father in heaven with Him. I have no doubt that one day we will get to meet up again. Even though, at the time of his death, I didn't get the affirmation I wanted, God is good, and He gave it to me later. While my father was in that coma, he had made peace with God.

The comfort I received from God was twofold. One part was about my father's peace and the other was my healing. Somewhere in this time, God started to change my perceptions and experiences (or lack thereof) of my father's love for me, to the point where I suddenly realised that my memories were no longer a painful lack of love, but I saw all my father did through the eyes of his love for me. Although he had never told me to my face that he loved me, even to this day, I can feel his love for me. All the pain of rejection is completely gone. My childhood memories are all happy. Because of this, I know that God can do anything – even heal a relationship when one person is dead!

About the Author

Ruth Embery lives with her husband, Daisy the dog and two chickens ironically named Butter and Tandoori in the beautiful Dandenong Ranges outside Melbourne, Australia. She has a passion to see people healed, whole and living the life of abundant freedom that Jesus promises through increasing connection with God. Ruth unleashes that passion through speaking engagements, retreats, mentoring, as well as prayer ministry and online coaching. Her blog is another space where she shares further insights and understanding about the Kingdom of God and the life of abundance. Ruth can be contacted via www.ruthembery.com.

Also by Ruth Embery

Untruth: Exploring Truth in a Post Truth World comes with a warning. If you are looking for answers or proofs for set positions, either theologically or socially, you may not find them here. Rather, the purpose is to prompt the questions we often fail to ask; to create a place where aspects of faith and culture we take for granted as truth, or are prescribed to us as truth, are opened up for discussion and examination to determine whether they actually stand up to close scrutiny.

We live in an era where many seem to be throwing out much of what we have believed as truth or culturally acceptable in the past in exchange for something new and progressive. When there are so many voices shouting that their way is the only right way, it is vitally important that we reassess our foundations. Are we really standing on what we think we are? And are these foundations actually stable or sufficient for the way ahead?

Untruth explores these questions and others to help open the way for conversation, greater understanding and increased certainty around what we do believe is truth and, more importantly, why we believe it is truth.

Untruth: Exploring Truth in a Post Truth World can be purchased at www.voiceinththedark.org or through many other online book retailers.

About Voice in the Dark Publishing

Every one of us has a story. As Christians, our story is vitally important. The transforming power of Jesus Christ in our lives not only encourages others, but also glorifies Him. At Voice in the Dark, we are all about creating a space for your story to be told. It might be that you have a specific area in which you know God has touched your life and there is no going back, or you may have a longer work of His renewing over many aspects of your life. Either way, we'd love the opportunity to not only help you, but to inspire others, that Jesus might be glorified. You don't need to be a writer or have any particular skills, just a story you'd like to share. If this sounds like you, or you'd just like to know more, get in touch with us via www.voiceinthedark.org.

www.ingramcontent.com/pod-product-compliance
Lightning Source LLC
Chambersburg PA
CBHW070729020526
44107CB00077B/2287